THE FEEBLE MINDED IN NEW YORK

A REPORT PREPARED FOR THE

PUBLIC EDUCATION ASSOCIATION OF NEW YORK

By
ANNE MOORE, Ph.D.

Published by
THE STATE CHARITIES AID ASSOCIATION

SPECIAL COMMITTEE ON PROVISION FOR THE FEEBLE-MINDED

NEW YORK CITY
United Charities Building
105 East 22nd Street
June, 1911

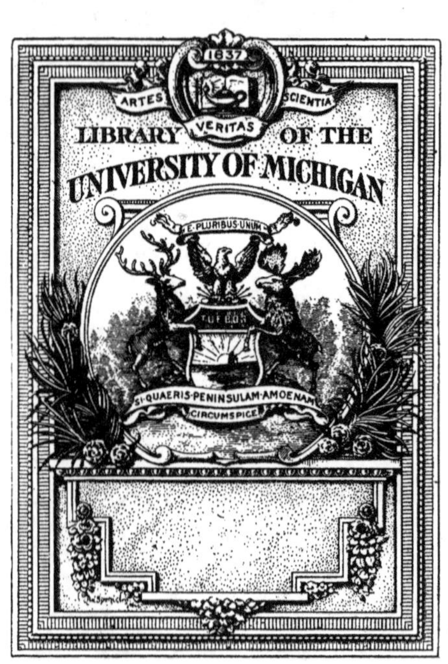
1837
ARTES
VERITAS
SCIENTIA
LIBRARY OF THE
UNIVERSITY OF MICHIGAN
E PLURIBUS UNUM
TUEBOR
SI QUAERIS PENINSULAM AMOENAM
CIRCUMSPICE

THE FEEBLE MINDED IN NEW YORK

A REPORT PREPARED FOR THE

PUBLIC EDUCATION ASSOCIATION OF NEW YORK

By

ANNE MOORE, Ph.D

Published by

THE STATE CHARITIES AID ASSOCIATION

SPECIAL COMMITTEE ON PROVISION FOR THE FEEBLE-MINDED

NEW YORK CITY
United Charities Building
105 East 22nd Street
June, 1911

Foreword

The following report represents an investigation into the conditions of the feeble-minded in New York City made by Dr. Anne Moore for the Public Education Association. This Association transmittted the report to the State Charities Aid Association with a request that further inquiry be made and some action taken. Accordingly, on April 21, 1911, the State Charities Aid Association organized a Special Committee on Provision for the Feeble-minded. This committee publishes the report of Dr. Moore. In giving publicity to the data set forth in the report the committee hopes to re-emphasize the fact that the feeble-minded are a growing danger and burden to society and that segregation can not only stop their reproduction but can also nearly extinguish their race. The committee proposes to collect further data and through legislation to provide means of completer segregation.

Dr. Walter B. James, *Chairman*

Hon. Homer Folks, *Secretary*

Dr. Felix Adler
Mrs. Joseph Allen
Mr. George F. Canfield
Miss M. V. Clark
Dr. L. Pierce Clark
Prof. C. B. Davenport
Hon. Michael J. Drummond
Mrs. M. C. Dunphy
Miss Elizabeth Farrell
Dr. Walter E. Fernald
Hon. Robert W. Hebberd
Miss Eleanor H. Johnson
Mr. E. R. Johnstone
Mr. Franklin B. Kirkbride
Mr. Sam A. Lewisohn
Mr. O. F. Lewis
Dr. William H. Maxwell
Dr. Frederick Peterson
Mr. Gustave Straubenmüller
Miss Marion R. Taber
Mr. Henry C. Wright

THE ARMY OF SORROW

Mary Butler Kirkbride

THERE ARE AT LEAST 200,000 PRONOUNCEDLY FEEBLE-MINDED PERSONS IN THE UNITED STATES. OF THESE 16,000 ARE INMATES OF ALMSHOUSES WHILE ONLY 18,000 ARE CARED FOR IN SPECIAL INSTITUTIONS.—*Fernald.*

MEN of victorious cities, aglow with the heat of the strife,
Men of the bountiful country, alert and throbbing with life,
Fathers of bright-eyed daughters, mothers of stalwart sons,
Hark to the host of the vanquished, marching with lowered guns.
For we are the Army of Sorrow, living, yet worse than dead,
Saddest of all God's creatures, from whom His light has fled.
The guilt of the mighty cities has doubled our teeming ranks,
But many a sun-lit valley sends stragglers at our flanks,
From village and town and prairie o'er the length and breadth of our land
Are gathered the thousands on thousands, who make up our pitiful band.
O God, can ye leave us longer, us who are guiltless of sin,
Or rest for a single moment till each lost sheep is within!
Gray-haired, yet catching at sunbeams; of age, yet playing with toys;
You house us with tramps and drunkards, grown men and man-grown boys.
Lured by each wayward impulse, bereft of the power of control,
Yet placed in a world of demons ready to snatch at our soul.
O Sisters, think of us women, children in innocence,
Yet mothers of fatherless babies, victims of foul offense.
Oh, the pangs that we must suffer, the anguish at their birth,
Hunted, and mocked, and branded the outcasts of the earth.
Saved only the bitter knowledge that by an iron law
Our children, and their children, must carry the self-same flaw.
O Brothers who hold the purse strings in each of the kindred states,
Who vote vast sums for highways, and decking of the gates,
If you laid the wealth of the nation in payment at our feet,
The debt to our lost manhood you still would fail to meet.
Yet now but a handful of us are guarded with zealous care,
While the rest, like a festering ulcer, on our country's breast lie bare.
If Love and fleet-foot Pity knock vainly at your door,
Shall Fear and Worldly-Wisdom not spur you on the more?
We ask for broad, green farm-lands, the sunshine that we love,
With stillness brooding o'er us like the wings of a nesting dove;
To taste the joys of labor on the lap of the kindly earth
And to prove, though maimed and halting, our lives may yet have worth.
We pray that each low ember you gently, wisely fan
Till each of us reach his measure of likeness to a man.
Your reward? May it not be the Vision that in our wrecked bodies of clay
A Christ-child was growing in wisdom and stature from day unto day?

—*Reprinted from The Survey of May* 6, 1911.

"Feeble-mindedness produces more pauperism, degeneracy and crime than any other one force. It touches every form of charitable activity. It is felt in every part of our land. It affects in some way all our people. Its cost is beyond our comprehension. It is the unappreciated burden of the unfortunate. It is a burden we are compelled to bear; therefore let us bear it intelligently to the end that the chain of evil may be lessened, the weak cared for, and the future made brighter with hope because of our efforts."

AMOS W. BUTLER, Conf. Char. & Cor. 1907.

CONTENTS

PART I

A STUDY OF FEEBLE-MINDED INDIVIDUALS AT LARGE IN NEW YORK

PART II

FEEBLE-MINDEDNESS AND WHAT IT MEANS

APPENDIX

PART I

A STUDY OF FEEBLE-MINDED INDIVIDUALS AT LARGE IN NEW YORK

Introduction

Though the problem of dealing effectively with the feeble-minded is intimately associated with the public welfare its immense importance has never been generally realized. The average citizen has no conception of the number of feeble-minded persons at large nor of the dangers attendant upon their unrestrained presence.

Those who have studied the question, however, realize that the feeble-minded are a menace to our present day civilization and that the problem of caring for them can no longer with safety be ignored. They agree that the defect is often hereditary and incurable, that it leads to poverty, degeneracy, crime and disease, and that the only way to deal with it effectively is to provide supervision and care that will last during the whole lifetime of the feeble-minded individual, certainly during the reproductive period.

A year ago the Public Education Association of New York began a study of the after-life of feeble-minded children who have been in the public schools. Specific facts were soon disclosed, so serious that it seemed wise to make an extended study of conditions due to the unrestrained presence of feeble-minded persons in the community. The results of this study are here presented in the hope that knowledge of the facts will lead to remedial measures and to a recognition of the necessity for appropriate legislation and adequate provision for the segregation of all feeble-minded persons.

My study of the situation in New York convinces me

(1) That the horrors attendant upon feeble-mindedness have, in no way, been exaggerated;

(2) That the condition is neither circumscribed nor local, though in New York City the price paid by the individual, his family, and the public at large is greater than in less crowded districts;

(3) That there is crying need for concerted action looking toward control of the situation.

It would be possible if sufficient time were given to the investigation to gather additional facts of the same character until the mass of evidence by its weight would convince the most skeptical.

Most of the individuals described in this study live in New York City, but a few reside elsewhere in the state. To secure their histories blanks were sent to the teachers of the ungraded classes in the public schools and to the out-of-town agents of the State Charities Aid Association; a study was made of the daily records of the Charity Organization Society and of the United Hebrew Charities, and conferences were held with individuals from whom information could be obtained. I have received many courtesies and I wish to express my thanks to all who have given me assistance.

These histories illustrate:

(1) The difficulty, under the present law and present state provision, of properly segregating defectives;

(2) Results that follow the unrestrained presence of the feebleminded in the community, such as demand upon family resources, upon normal strength, and upon charity; production of defective offspring; indulgence of immoral and criminal tendencies;

(3) The demand made upon the resources of the public schools of the city.

Feeble-minded Persons Supported by Charity

Feeble-mindedness contributes greatly to the problem of relief work, and constitutes a serious drain upon the resources of all agencies for relief, public and private. Case after case comes up where the cause of dependency is directly traceable to family taint. To prevent suffering material aid must be given, and under existing conditions it can not be given in such a way as to react toward the permanent benefit of the individual. Resources which should be used for the relief of normal persons are diverted to the need of defectives and the result is that conditions which should be made impossible are perpetuated.

The two following cases are striking instances of the difficulty experienced by the various charity organizations and by the Department of Charities in dealing with the feeble-minded. An enormous amount of trouble has been taken to help these women but in neither case has any permanent good resulted.

MINNIE H.

This woman is thirty-four years of age She is morally weak, mentally incapable of the industrial efficiency necessary to earn her living and physically weak. In 1897 she married a man 13 years her senior, like herself, an American of Irish extraction and a member of the Roman Catholic Church. He was a heavy drinker and had once attempted suicide. In 1898 a girl was born. In the same year the husband became insane and was committed to the Manhattan State Hospital. In 1899 he was discharged to his wife. In 1901 a second girl was born. In the same year the husband again became insane and was committed to the Manhattan State Hospital for the second time. He is at present in the State Hospital at Central Islip.

To the children the mother brought even a worse inheritance than the father. Her mother died on Blackwell's Island from the effects of hard drinking. Her father is an alcoholic, a loafer and irresponsible. A sister is an imbecile and is at present in the Newark Asylum. A brother is insane from drinking and smoking to excess and is now in the Manhattan State Hospital. The double taint of alcoholism, insanity, and feeble-mindedness has told upon the children. The older child has adenoids and enlarged tonsils and is weak physically; the younger has adenoids, enlarged tonsils, chorea and is sub-normal mentally.

The family has always lived from hand to mouth with occasional help from neighbors. After the husband was removed to the Hospital the woman's mother, father and sister came to live with her. The case was then brought to the attention of the Charity Organization Society. On investigation it was found that the woman had secured work as a domestic for $12 a month, with hours from 12 A. M. to 9 P. M. The children were left during her absence from home in charge of the drunken grandmother. At the mother's request the children were committed by the city to a Home, but within a year they were discharged without proper investigation, the older to the mother, the younger to the drunken grandmother. Later they were found covered with vermin, ill-nourished, living in two badly ventilated, ill-lighted rooms. The mother was at this time working as a cleaner in a theatre at $7 a week, but she had to give up her situation because she became pregnant as the result of illicit relations with a man she met in the theatre.

The Charity Organization Society assumed charge of the woman's affairs, stored her furniture, saw that the children were provided for, and found a place for her in the New York Infant Asylum. It was intended to place by adoption the child that was born there but while efforts were pending the baby died of spinal meningitis. Work was found for the woman at the Infant Asylum and she remained there with the younger girl for several months. During this time the older child was kept in a Home at the city's expense. While at the asylum the woman proved that under supervision she could work well and remain industrious and sober, but that she did not have the moral strength to stand alone. After various vicissitudes she expressed the wish to have a home and have her children with her, and the Charity Organization Society secured rooms for her and installed her and the children in them. She was sent to the Manhattan Trade School and was regularly paid for her apprentice work in the hope that she would become self-supporting, but she was unable to hold a position after leaving the school. For some time she was given monthly her rent and $2, and clothes were furnished for her and the children. In addition she was paid weekly $3.50 in wages which she could not and did not earn. This aid amounted in 1908 to $185 and in 1909 to $133. The cash outlay however, represents the smallest part of the expenditure.

In the Appendix, page 122, is given in abbreviated form the daily record of assistance given this woman by the Charity Organization Society. A glance will show the great amount of normal energy that has gone to waste in trying to fit her for a place in the world and keep her from actual suffering. In addition she has taxed the resources and ingenuity of the St. Vincent de Paul Society, the parish, various friends, several hospitals, several dispensaries, and other city institutions. Commitment at the proper time would have resulted in an enormous saving of money and of vital strength that should not have been spent unproductively. It would have prevented the bringing into the world of three unfit children, and it would have resulted in turning a wasteful drag upon society into a useful member of it, contributing largely to her own support.

Sarah P.

This woman is mentally unbalanced and is also afflicted with tuberculosis and heart disease. She is married to a man with cancer. They have one idiot son, two feeble-minded sons, and an apparently normal daughter. The parents are Russian Jews. When they arrived in this country in 1897 the idiot boy, Harry, was nine years old, and one of the feeble-minded boys, Sam, was a year old. The other feeble-minded boy, Leon, was born in 1899.

For years this family has been a burden to the United Hebrew Charities and to the Department of Charities. The mother has played one of these organizations off against the other and has been able to bend both to her will. The story is told in the record of assistance given her by the United Hebrew Charities (Appendix, page 137). She takes the ground that the United Hebrew Charities owes her a living and manages to secure about $25 monthly. At various times she has had the children committed to Randall's Island and other institutions. As soon as the United Hebrew Charities, finding that she is unencumbered, attempts to cut down the amount furnished her she demands from the Department of Charities that the children be discharged. When she has the children again she demands from the United Hebrew Charities the full amount on the ground that she is a widow with four children and can not be expected to get along with less.

To treat the woman like a normal person and refuse to comply with her demands unless she follows a certain course of action would result in undoubted suffering both on her part and on the part of the children. The case is a remarkable illustration of the inadvisability of leaving the disposition of feeble-minded children in the hands of parents who are themselves abnormal and utterly unfit to determine what is best for themselves, for the children, or for the community, as the following record of commitments and discharges will show.

The idiot son, Harry, was admitted to Randall's Island, Aug. 16, 1901, and discharged May 28, 1903; he was again admitted March 16, 1906, and discharged April 16, 1906. In February, 1905, Sam, one of the feeble-minded boys, was admitted to Randall's Island, but was discharged almost immediately. The other feeble-minded boy, Leon, was admitted March 16, 1906, and was discharged April 14, 1906. May 21, application was made for the commitment of Sam and Hannah, the girl. Leon was sent to Randall's Island again and on February 13, 1907, application was made for his discharge. Later Leon was recommitted to Randall's Island. He was discharged to the Gerry Society on March 16, 1910. February 18, 1910, Sam was committed to Randall's Island and the mother sent to Bellevue, as mentally unbalanced. She was almost immediately discharged.

Feeble-minded Women of Child-bearing Age

"Feeble-minded women are sources of debauchery and licentiousness which pollute the lives of boys and youth of the community, disseminate disease, and bring young children into the world destined to repeat their history."[1]

At large and unrestrained, feeble-minded women are subject to overwhelming temptations that lead them toward sexual immorality. The tendency asserts itself even in the school room where frequently, in spite of the vigilance of teachers, feeble-minded girls become centers of corruption. Feeble-minded women are likely to give birth to large numbers of children which in spite of a high rate of mortality survive in considerable numbers. Again and again these women return to maternity hospitals[2] where the best medical skill is at their disposal to insure their safety, and the safe delivery of offspring that stands every chance of being imbecile, degenerate or criminal, and that sooner or later will come to be a burden upon the public.

It is a short-sighted policy, penny-wise and pound-foolish, which does not provide adequately for the segregation of feeble-minded women. It is estimated that the institution at Newark (capacity 795) has saved the state the birth of at least 5,000 defective children. If the potential reproductive power of feeble-minded children and their potential degeneracy is considered it must be conceded that the cost of this institution has been more than offset by the saving effected by it.

FRIEDA S.

Frieda S. is 37 years old, of German extraction. She is partially paralyzed, has a deformed head, shows slight mental enfeeblement, and is quarrelsome, wild, intemperate. She married a man of the same age, of Irish extraction. He is intemperate, epileptic, tubercular, feeble-minded. The eighth child was born in February, 1910. The seven other children died in infancy from neglect and starvation. The couple has been a charge upon the resources of the C. O. S.;

[1]W. E. Fernald.

[2]The Superintendent of one of our largest maternity hospitals estimates that of the feeble-minded women treated there at least 95% are cases following rape.

the A. I. C. P.; the S. P. C. C.; the Salvation Army; St. Jerome's church; St. Elizabeth's Society; the Soc. St. Vincent de Paul; the maternity wards of various hospitals.

When the last child was born the Charity Organization Society, feeling that the baby would die from neglect as the other babies died, while the woman was still in Bellevue hospital made an effort to get her committed to some institution. The following letters were written.

"My dear Dr. ——: F. S. is in the maternity ward of Bellevue Hospital. Her baby was born about ten days ago. She is paralytic and has been on the records of this society since 1908. She has borne eight children all of whom died when young. Her husband and she have been vagabonds most of the time since the case came on record. Both are now about 37 years old and they have no home. We find them living with the man's father who is being supported by a pension from two charitable ladies who refuse to have this couple live with the old man. This couple both drink and neither have ever been known to work; the woman of course, in her paralytic condition is unable to work. Is there any possible chance of having her cared for in an institution with her child after she comes out of Bellevue? Otherwise, she will try to find shelter wherever she can with the child, and the baby will die in a short time. If there could be a commitment made while she is still in the hospital, it might be a good thing for her, in taking her off the charity of private individuals and placing her where she properly belongs. Will you kindly give this matter your attention and let me know what can be done for her. Very truly yours, ——."

"My dear ——: Replying to your letter of the 11th inst. relative to F. S. She is now at the maternity ward of Bellevue Hospital. I beg to state that although she shows some slight mental enfeeblement she is not a proper case for custodial care in any sense of the word. Owing to her paralyzed condition she may not be able to take care of herself, but I doubt whether she can be sent to any custodial institution for care except the almshouse. Very truly yours, ——."

The S. P. C. C. replied to a similar communication as follows:

"My dear ——: I do not see just what can be done in this case. There is not sufficient legal ground to remove the child. If you will inform the Society when the woman is discharged from Bellevue Hospital and of the address to which she goes, I shall see that special attention is given the case with the view that immediate action be taken should conditions at any time indicate that she is not a proper guardian."

No advantage could be taken of this offer for on inquiry it was found that she had been discharged from Bellevue Hospital to an unknown person claiming to be a cousin who left no address.

JENNIE E.

A girl of 18 years, a low grade imbecile. Her parents are Russian Jews. Her mother was frightened by a terrible fire before her birth. The family of five live on $7 a week in 3 poor rooms. The girl is utterly incapable of doing housework or anything else. She has been in the ungraded class, but she was unable to learn anything. She cannot write her name, she cannot even copy letters that are made for her, nor count the strokes of a pencil up to five. Her mother wants her at home but would consent to having the girl sent to an institution in order to be rid of the constant nervous strain of her presence. She would prefer to have the girl marry. The girl is in the habit of meeting in Seward Park the feeble-minded boys whom she knew in the ungraded class.

ELLA A.

Girl fourteen years old. On March 3, 1908, she was reported as having stolen a watch from some one in the school room; the watch was recovered and no prosecution followed. Her school records are unfavorable; deportment and lessons poor. On April 14, 1908, she was arrested with two boys, one aged 12 and the other aged 11, charged with grand larceny. She was tried and acquitted. The investigation showed that the girl was very fond of the company of boys and had been seen going into the basement and on the roofs of houses with them. The parents seemed indifferent to the matter. The case was continued under investigation for a considerable period during which conditions improved in the home. Naturally the teacher of this girl feels keenly the responsibility of having her in school.

NELLIE S.

Girl 14 years old, feeble-minded, immoral. Her father and mother are cousins. There are eleven children in this family, not one of whom is normal. A sister is insane; a sister feeble-minded on Randall's Island; a brother feeble-minded, has been in the House of Refuge. This girl, when eleven years old, was in the City Hospital on Ward's Island with venereal disease. She can do work if constantly supervised; she is now in the needle-craft school, but is erratic and often destroys material wantonly.

Mary B.

Girl of 17, native, of Irish parentage, a congenital imbecile. Her father and mother are alcoholic. The family of nine live in three tiny, unsanitary rooms on from $2 to $10 a week. The children are ill-fed, ill-clothed, neglected, constantly sick and constantly asking aid. The imbecile girl tends the baby and does the family washing; otherwise, she roams the streets. She is capable of employment if placed in proper surroundings. In 1908, through the efforts of the Charity Organization Society, papers were made out for her admission to Newark with the consent of the parents. They were, however, sent by the Department of Public Charities to the house and left there. When the mother saw that details concerning the family were recorded she withdrew her consent to having the girl put away.

Miriam R.

This woman is a chronic habitué of dispensaries. She has been treated for hysteria, heart disease, neurasthenia, prolapsus of the womb, varicose veins, tuberculosis, acute rheumatism. She is slightly feeble-minded. Her sister and her sister's son are slightly feeble-minded. Her husband is an incapable. Five children are living; one is dead, and another is expected. A son of 18 is imbecile. He is physically healthy, cannot work, roams the streets and has bad personal habits. A daughter of 16 is feeble-minded. She is able to help her mother about the house, but she is of the age when she needs supervision that the mother is incapable of giving. She has eczema, defective teeth, and nasal catarrh. The entire family suffers from malnutrition. They are supported in part by the United Hebrew Charities, and besides gifts of food and clothing they receive on an average $6 monthly.

Mamie S.

Girl of fifteen years, an imbecile who should be under custodial care. In February, 1909, she set on fire a younger sister who was a paralytic and the child was burned to death. Application was made for her admission to Newark through the efforts of the Charity Organization Society, but a physician to whom the mother appealed advised her to withdraw her consent and the plan to commit the girl fell through. The grandmother insists that the girl is well cared for and that under no condition will consent be given to send her to Newark. The family lives under wretched conditions. When the last baby was born the basement was found flooded with dirty water from a leak in the sewer, and gas was escaping from a leak in the pipe. The midwife, afraid of losing her case, did not wish to have these conditions reported. The father is alcoholic and has been arrested for desertion and non-support. He beats his wife, uses vile language and is not a fit person to have the charge of children. The mother is weak and ignorant. She has had eleven children, all of whom are defective. The oldest girl is in a very low physical condition and is a moral imbecile. She is out at night until twelve o'clock, is troublesome and beyond control. Three years ago a policeman in Corlears Park made an effort to have her put away for her own good. The mother objected because she felt the girl would be useful at home in caring for the younger children during her coming confinement. She finally gave her consent to have the girl sent away for a year, and through the S. P. C. C. she was sent to the House of the Good Shepherd. Two years later she was at home but was unhappy, and in February, 1910, she ran away. She was supposed to be married, but in a month she was back again. Her whereabouts while she was away are unknown. Lately the family has moved from place to place in order to escape investigation by the S. P. C. C.

YETTA E.

Girl 14 years old. Imbecile, has trachoma, is guilty of self-abuse. Her mother is feeble-minded and immoral; her father is alcoholic; her sister is a moral imbecile; her brother is an imbecile; two cousins are feeble-minded.

LILLIE W., Oneida Co., N. Y.

Woman of 23, feeble-minded. Both father and mother are feeble-minded. There has been constant inter-marriage in the family. She has nine brothers all of whom are wild and backward. All except one have been arrested, usually for stealing; they use vile language and are known to be immoral. The woman has one illegitimate child. She does not know who the father is, but it is supposed to be her brother. The child was taken from the mother by the court and placed in a local home, but she was so bad mentally and morally that she could not be kept with the other children. She is now in Syracuse. The mother was sent for a time to a correctional institution. She is now at large, keeping house for some man.

EDNA M., Oneida Co., N. Y.

Woman of 38, feeble-minded, moral imbecile. She married and had two legitimate children. She left her husband and went to live with his brother who is feeble-minded. She bore four illegitimate children, two of whom are feeble-minded. The last child was born in the Oneida County Home. All six of the children have syphilis. Five of them are in the Home of the Good Shepherd, Utica. The woman is now at large.

MILLIE M., Amsterdam, N. Y.

Girl 19, epileptic and feeble-minded; native, her father is Irish, her mother Scotch. Her father is alcoholic and is in States Prison for incest. Her mother is sub-normal mentally. Her sister, 17 years old, is in a House of Refuge. She has an illegitimate child by her father.

KATIE T., Troy, N. Y.

Girl of 19, high grade imbecile and a moral imbecile. Her father is alcoholic, her mother immoral. She was for a time in an orphan asylum, later in the Hudson Training School. She was paroled. Afterwards she became pregnant. She cannot be sent back to the Training School as she is over age.

ANNIE L., Troy, N. Y.

Feeble-minded girl, has been waiting for months for entrance to Syracuse. Her mother, intemperate and immoral, is now in the almshouse with paralytic stroke. The girl is nearing 14 and may lose her chance to enter the institution.

GRACE N., Poughkeepsie, N. Y.

Girl of 18. She has bad heredity and has lived in a bad environment. She spends her time between the city and county almshouses and the county jail. She has several illegitimate children.

Families Burdened by Feeble-minded Children

To sensitive people the presence of a feeble-minded child in the home involves so much shame, anxiety and grief that he becomes an intolerable burden. To care for him properly consumes the energy and vitality of some one who might otherwise be a productive member of society. The earnings of a family may be so depleted in this way that the family becomes a charge upon public or private charity. If the mother is the wage-earner normal children may be pressed into service to care for the defective child to the detriment of their health and education. If the mother is governed by especial maternal tenderness for the weakling she is apt in her effort to care for him to overtax her strength and consequently to neglect the normal children who, as a result, lose much of their chance to become useful citizens. Such a mother is least likely to realize that her duty is to care for the normal children and yield the defective child to the care of the state. Proper provision for segregation would relieve her of the burden of an unwise decision to care for the weakling herself.

Shiftless people sometimes regard the feeble-minded child as an asset, for his infirmity may be successfully exploited. He is sent out to beg or he is set to work in the hope that he may add a few dollars to the family income. Often he suffers from cruelty or neglect, often he is made to care for normal children who suffer from being left to his mercy.

VINCENT C.

Boy of eleven years, native, of Irish parentage. He has a large, flat head, foolish eyes, and open mouth. He cannot speak, nor understand what is said. He cannot walk, he cannot raise himself if seated on the floor. He sits all day in a chair shaking his body, moving his hands and giggling foolishly. The mother is busy all day caring for him and gets out very little. He has been taken to "St. Anne's Relic" and his mother believes he was benefited. She objects to having him go to an institution because of tales she has heard, but when he is eighteen she says she will consent, if he is still troublesome. The mother was not properly attended to at the birth of her first child as she depended on an inefficient midwife. She has borne four other children, and has had five miscarriages. Three of the children died in infancy, the fourth has migraine and her speech is defective.

FANNIE L.

Girl, native, imbecile. Her father is alcoholic and has stomach trouble; her mother is alcoholic; her brother has catarrh and his hearing is defective; her sister is physically degenerate; another sister is feeble-minded. The girl's eyes and head are abnormal. She has marasmus, is ill-nourished, ill-clad and neglected. Her muscles are unco-ordinated. She feeds the baby with anything it will swallow. The family is dependent on charity for subsistence.

CLARE G.

Girl of ten, an imbecile of too low a grade to be admitted to the ungraded classes of the public schools. In appearance she is horrible. Her condition is probably due to syphilitic inheritance. Her father is a wealthy Jew and he refuses to pay for proper institution care.

LOUIE C.

Boy of twelve years; native, of Irish parentage. The mother is alcoholic and abuses the children. The older sister is kept home from school to care for the boy. He is an epileptic and too feeble-minded for admission to the ungraded classes. He has had convulsions and abscesses, and lost his right eye in an accident. He is vicious, is likely to injure himself and others, and runs the streets. He should be in an institution, but his parents hold him for the sympathy he draws.

NORA D.

A helpless girl who was afflicted with hydrocephalus as the result of brain fever and spinal meningitis when about a year old. She finally degenerated into a mass of flesh, just able to swallow the food that was put into her mouth. She was the third of six children, the two oldest of whom are married. The parents were American Protestants, the mother is neurasthenic, the father is dead. The mother has supported the family while the grandmother eared for Nora. The three younger children were neglected, became nervous and anaemic, and irregular in their attendance at school. After the grandmother died the care of the afflicted child devolved upon the younger children who had to be kept out of school for the purpose. The mother resisted every effort to have Nora placed in some custodial institution, even the effort to place the other children temporarily in a convalescent home. Nora died last winter at the age of eighteen.

Mildred L.

Girl of ten years, feeble-minded, very low grade. She is kept out of school to care for the baby. The family is under the care of a charitable society. The father is alcoholic and has spent six months in the workhouse; he has rheumatism and is feeble-minded. He runs an elevator. The mother is alcoholic. There are three other children.

Harry C.

A boy eight years old; of native Dutch parentage. The home is comfortable. A congenital feeble-minded case, the head in bad condition when born. His speech is defective, he is neurotic, has had tics, is constantly moving. He must be cared for like a baby. He was on Randall's Island from November, 1909, to January, 1910. His parents were dissatisfied with his treatment and withdrew him.

Willie W.

Boy 14 years old, native, of Irish parentage. His home is comfortable. He faints easily, has had ricketts, enlarged tonsils, adenoids, and has been circumcised because of self-abuse. He drags his feet, has vacant eyes and hanging jaw, and is nervous and excitable. His speech is defective and he talks constantly. He is very unclean in his bodily habits and eats anything he can put in his mouth, especially the buttons from his clothes. He is an imbecile, unable to wash or dress himself, and incapable of learning to read and write. Some years ago he was in the public school, but he was abused and maltreated by the other children, and unable to defend himself. He is now too wild and his habits too unclean for school. For a time he was on Randall's Island, but his mother withdrew him.

Lizzie Z.

Girl of seven years; native, of German parentage, living in poor surroundings. She was injured at birth, is hydrocephalic, and utterly helpless. She has had diphtheria and measles, and the right side of her body is paralyzed so that the right leg is drawn up and cannot be straightened. Her eyes roll helplessly and she can distinguish only light from darkness. She moans constantly. The mother thinks her teeth ache and wants them extracted. She is eager for food, recognizes the rattle of dishes, and is fed with the family fare. Although caring for her taxes the mother's strength to the utmost, she is too much afraid of what the neighbors will say to make an effort to put the child away.

Albert L.

Boy eleven years old; native, of Russian Jewish parentage. The family of eight live in three rooms under very poor conditions. The boy had brain fever in infancy. He is idiotic, absolutely irresponsible, and unable to do anything. He cannot match pictures. He crawls up and down stairs like a baby and eats anything —garbage, paste, crayon. It is manifestly bad for normal children to be exposed to free contact with such defectives.

Silas M.

Boy fifteen years old; native. His father was German, his mother Swedish. His home is comfortable. His father had syphilis, took morphine, went insane and finally committed suicide. His mother is abnormal and too much out of sympathy with the boy to provide the right sort of care for him. One sister is epileptic. The boy is an epileptic. He has had brain fever, meningitis, pneumonia, measles, and whooping-cough. When five years old he fell and struck his head and was unconscious for some time. He is slightly feeble-minded, sullen, violent at times, and uses very bad language. He is a chronic vagrant. About a year ago he was committed to Craig Colony, but after a few months he ran away in one of his moments of excitement. He was found after some weeks of searching, for which his family could ill-afford to pay. He has been twice on Randall's Island; once he was ill-advisedly withdrawn by the mother. The second time he was sent to Craig Colony. The authorities feel that they can do nothing further for him, for to send him to Craig again will but result in a repetition of the above experience. There is nothing ahead of this boy but criminality, unless he can be placed where he will receive proper training and supervision. His presence in the home is sapping the vitality of his mother and three sisters, and the antagonistic influence of his surroundings is aggravating the boy's condition. Again and again he has run away and usually, after days of search, he is found in a filthy, unkempt condition in some stable, in association with men unfit mentally or morally to care for him.

William L.

Boy, born in 1899, in Roumania; an imbecile. Arrived in the United States in 1900. In Randall's Island, 1907, but was removed by mother who states that she believed he had been badly treated. He is a hopeless case, but nothing could be done for him as his mother would not consent to having him sent to Randall's Island again.

Feeble-minded Persons Allowed to Marry

Morbid heredity is the strongest factor in producing feeble-mindedness. If one parent is afflicted with a neuropathic taint the probability is that one or more of the children will be feeble-minded. If this taint is strengthened by neuropathic taint in the other parent, or by some other contributory factor such as tuberculosis or alcoholism, the chances for defective offspring are increased. If both parents are feeble-minded the strong probability is that all the children will be feeble-minded. In the light of the recognized hereditary character of mental defect more care should be exercised than is done at present in the granting of marriage licenses. It has been suggested that a marriage law should be passed requiring a clean bill of health and evidence of normal mind before a license is issued. If persons afflicted with syphilis or with gonorrhoea were not allowed to marry and if restrictive measures were established preventing people with morbid inheritance from having children, the number of the feeble-minded would speedily be reduced; for it has been estimated that 90 per cent of the defect is traceable to this cause.

PHILIP Z.

In 1906 a school principal wrote to a member of the Child Labor committee asking assistance in the case of a feeble-minded boy. Her letter in part is as follows:

"Although fifteen, he cannot go to work because he can produce no proof of age, and cannot meet the scholastic requirements. He will never be able to do either as long as he lives. He is a defective of the very lowest type and is subject to attacks which are almost insanity, and are sometimes accompanied by violence. After a year of hard work and patient teaching, Miss —— reports that he can barely write his name; can make change if he has money but cannot perform the necessary processes if he has no money. Can sometimes read in a primer, but not always even that.

"Not one of the family is normal. The best we could discover of the father was that he had been sent to the insane asylum on Ward's Island. The mother is almost idiotic, and is living with a man to whom she is not married. There is a baby almost ten months old, but whether it is this man's child or not I cannot find out. This man has precipitated the present difficulty by putting Philip out of the house, saying that a boy of his age and size must go to work. Where Philip is now we do not know, although he has been seen on the streets at night. Of course we can get him back to school eventually; but the question is what shall we do with him and for him when we get him.

"I can see only three possible solutions, with grave difficulties in the way of each. They are:

"(1) To let him go to work, since he is physically able to earn enough to support himself. The objections, present and future, to this are obvious.

"(2) To give him a scholarship until he is sixteen. That will only postpone the final settlement of his case, however.

"(3) To confine him in the home for children of his type in Randall's Island. That means a tedious process, in the course of which the boy is almost sure to disappear, especially as he is not lacking in a certain street shrewdness, and views every new person he meets with suspicion. He ran out of school screaming madly, one day last spring, and was gone for days, because a chance visitor spoke to him.

"Our information has been obtained from neighbors, by visits to the home made by Miss —— and the school doctor. In the course of the year we have clothed him and fed him a great part of the time, have sent baskets of provisions to the family several times when we found them in dire need. Of course we cannot keep this up. There are too many other calls, and I feel that the time has come for decisive action."

The boy secured a marriage license and is now married.[1]

---

[1] Other striking instances of the marriage of feeble-minded persons are described under various headings in this report.

Feeble-minded Immigrants Not Deported

The large number of cases of feeble-mindedness to be found among our foreign population suggests that greater care should be exercised by the authorities in admitting feeble-minded immigrants or immigrants likely to give birth to feeble-minded children. The following cases illustrate the character of feeble-minded parents and children occasionally admitted by the immigration officers. These are but two of many cases that might be used to illustrate the need of greater care at our entry ports.

Ysik K.

Boy of ten, Russian Jew. His parents are cousins; they are now separated. He has an epileptic uncle. The boy has epilepsy, enlarged tonsils, and is possibly insane. He was given poppy seed when a baby to keep him quiet. He is guilty of self-abuse; runs the streets. He was excluded from the ungraded class as untrainable, irresponsible, ugly and dangerous. He was on Randall's Island from April to July, 1909, but he was removed because there was danger of his being deported, as he had, too soon after admission to the country, become a charge upon the state.

Donato M.

Feeble-minded boy, twelve years old. He exhibits a strong immoral tendency; is brutal to others weaker than himself; is an inveterate crap player. This child has been treated most brutally by his mother who is married to a man who has been sent to prison for two years for assault.

On the passport from Italy this boy and his brother, who is also feeble-minded, are described as "natural," and the ages given are several years more than those on the christening certificate, which are evidently the proper ages. This case has been referred twice to the Children's Society which is investigating it.

Note by the Committee.—The above two cases are but illustrative of cases that have not been excluded by our emigration officials. From the partial statistics thus far gathered it appears to the Committee to be conclusive that there are a large number of feeble-minded among the immigrants. The Committee will make investigations along this line during the coming year and will be able to present thereafter fuller data.

Feeble-minded Persons Guilty of Arson

Arson is a common crime among the feeble-minded. They like the excitement attendant upon a fire and wantonly set fires for no other motive than the pleasure of seeing the engines turn out and watching the flames. Many times thousands of dollars worth of property are destroyed and many lives endangered before legal proof of guilt is established. On conviction these persons are often committed to penal institutions, only to be paroled and set free to repeat the crime; or they are left to serve long sentences which on their release do not act as a deterrent. The Fire Marshal of New York City tells me that a sufficient number of cases of pyromania have come to his atttention to fill a special institution.

Two cases have come to my knowledge in which feeble-minded children have set fire to the clothing of other children with fatal consequences. Such fatalities have often resulted from the custom of allowing children to build bonfires in the street and to dance at will about the flames.

THOMAS T.

Between the dates February 1, 1910, and July 12, 1910, sixteen fires occurred in the district bounded by Fifth and Lexington avenues and 108th and 119th streets, all in twenty-family, five-story tenements, and all of similar incendiary origin. These fires were traced to a feeble-minded youth who had no motive for the deed except a desire for excitement. When he visited one of the buildings to deliver goods his method was to light a bundle of papers which he had previously saturated with kerosene from a bottle which he carried with him, and leave them in the hallway, in a corner of the stairway, or in the cellar. He was caught and convicted on the sixteenth fire. He was declared insane and is now confined in the Central Islip State Hospital.

HENRY Y.

A feeble-minded man, 25 years of age, started 45 fires within three months. The loss was estimated at a quarter of a million dollars. He usually left something burning in the airshaft or wood-bin.

At his trial he was declared sane and was sent to Elmira. After 13 months he was released on parole and won his absolute release. He is now working in a hospital in Newark, N. J.

Paul X.

A feeble-minded boy, living in Massachusetts, set fire to his grandfather's house. He saved himself by jumping from the upper window into a cherry tree. Afterwards, he set fire to a stable in Gloucester, Mass., and was sent to a reform school for two and a half years. After his release he set on fire, one by one, a row of houses owned by different clergymen, called "holy row." Later he burned a house belonging to the father of the district attorney, was caught, and convicted. He spent four years in Charlestown Prison. He became religious and was paroled on condition that he go to another state. He came to New York and for a time was under Mrs. Booth's care. Afterwards he set fire to a barn and to the Bayside Yacht Club. He was caught and convicted. He is now in Sing Sing.

Peter S.

Extract from the *New York Times:*

"Detective Reemey was in hiding last night near the home of 16-year-old P—— S——, at — E. 214th Street, the Bronx. He had been there since last Wednesday night feeling pretty sure that the boy would come along. The boy lives at the 214th Street number with his father; his mother is dead. Shortly after 8 o'clock, Reemey saw a figure creep up to the back door of the S—— home and knock at the door. The detective pounced on him, locking him up on the charge of juvenile delinquency.

"Last Wednesday night young S—— was with a crowd of boys around a bonfire at 214th Street and White Plains Road. According to their ethics, no boy could stand at the bonfire unless he gathered some of the wood that was necessary to keep it going. Any newcomer who brought with him some wood was welcome; one who insisted on enjoying the sight of the leaping flames and the warmth without bringing wood was an interloper.

"Thirteen-year-old Fioro Bernardo of 3827 Carpenter avenue, added himself to the crowd around the fire. Some said later that he had brought wood; others denied it. Anyway young S—— set upon him, it is charged, poured a bottle of kerosene over his head, and then threw him into the fire. The other boys dragged him out of the fire, tore off his clothes and ran in search of a policeman. The lad, who was badly burned all over, was removed to the Fordham Hospital. It was said there last night that he was in a serious condition and might not live.

"The S—— boy told Detective Reemey that he did not know that the liquid in the bottle he had poured over Fioro's head was kerosene; he thought it was only water, he said. Reemey found, however, that S—— had brought the bottle from his own home and used part of the kerosene to start the fire, showing that he knew very well what was in it. He has already spent two years in the Catholic Protectory, to which he was sent on a truancy charge."

This boy was examined by a physician who diagnosed the case as one of mental defect. The boy was arraigned in the Children's Court November 18, 1910, and, after a full examination, committed to the New York Catholic Protectory.

Feeble-minded Children in the Public Schools

No legal provision is made in our public schools for mental defectives. The Compulsory Education Law in spirit recognizes that every child is entitled to receive an education, and that no child shall be discriminated against because of physical or mental disability; but, curiously, it exempts from school attendance children who are "physically or mentally unfit," though such children most need to have their small powers developed. Whether they will send their defective children to school or not, is, therefore, optional with the parents.

Recognizing, however, that the presence of sub-normal children in regular grades seriously interferes with the progress of their normal fellows and that such children need special training which can not be given in the regular grades, the Board of Education has established special ungraded classes for children who can not keep up with the regular grades.

Defective children are reported by school principals to the Inspector of Ungraded Classes. They are then examined by a physician and, if the diagnosis warrants it, they are assigned to an ungraded class. In this way the most extreme cases of idiocy and imbecility have been removed from the regular class rooms; but many borderline cases remain which teachers, lacking the expert knowledge necessary to interpret the signs of abnormality, fail to recognize. A year or two ago out of 370 principals in Manhattan, the Bronx, and Richmond, 168 failed to report any children not making normal progress. This indicates either serious inability to recognize mental defect or an indifference to the subject.

Feeble-minded Children in Ungraded Classes

One hundred and twenty-five ungraded classes have been established in Greater New York and in them about 2,000 defective children are cared for. The majority of these classes are in the most congested districts of the city where the worst conditions prevail. The children are therefore mostly of foreign parents and live in tenements, usually under poor conditions. In mentality they vary from the backward child, who, under proper conditions may make a grade, to the helpless idiot; in appearance, from the pathetic vacuity of dulled faculties to the repulsiveness of deformity. In the classes a series of tests determines the grade and character of training that may be advantageously given. As a result of training, these children improve in articulation, in muscular control and in the use of their benumbed faculties. This training should not be allowed to lapse, as it does under present conditions, when the children leave school. If it were continued under proper supervision many of these children could be made useful and happy, and at least partially self-supporting.

A proper segregation law would remove from these classes the following hampering conditions:

(1) Lack of power to enforce attendance upon defective children who might profit by special training.
(2) Lack of provision to continue the training of defective children after they have reached the school age limit of 16.
(3) Overcrowding of the classes with cases that properly belong in custodial institutions, to the detriment of the interests of the less backward children.
(4) Unintelligent opposition.

The facts in the following table were secured through the courtesy and generous co-operation of Miss Elizabeth Farrell, Inspector of Ungraded Classes, and the teachers of these classes. The histories of 317 cases representing 32 classes were furnished me. Of the 317 cases, 206 are male, 111 are female; 40 are native Americans, 277 are of foreign parentage. Of these, 130 are of Jewish parentage (Russian or Austrian), 40 Italian, 35 German, 20 Irish, 9 negro. The others are of Bohemian, Bulgarian, Swedish, Norwegian, Scotch, Swiss, Hungarian, English, Canadian, parentage. They represent all degrees of mental defect and, except in one case, are between the ages of 7 and 17. The cause of the defect may be variously traced in individual cases to mental defect, disease, or alcoholism in the parents; to infantile diseases or injury in infancy; to poverty and malnutrition, and to combinations of all these conditions. The number of children in the families varies from 2 to 13. The majority of the cases have immoral habits, or tendencies which must of necessity have a deleterious effect upon other children with whom they come in contact. The number of cases is too small to permit of percentages, and the individual histories are incomplete, but the aggregate of facts discloses a condition which warrants serious attention.

TABLE A

One Hundred Cases of Feeble-Minded Children at Present in the Ungraded Classes of the Public Schools of Greater New York, Taken at Random from 317 Cases

(Abbreviations: m, male; f, female; f.m, feeble-minded; poor means income less than living wage; good, living wage or more; bad means poor, plus bad sanitation and bad influences; tb, tuberculosis. A blank means that no information has been obtained.)

A. Case	Sex	Age	Home	Family	Characteristics
1	m	14	Poor; 10 in 4 rooms.	8 children; 6 abnormal.	Self-abuse; easily influenced.
2	m	13	Poor; 6 in 4 rooms.	2 children, both fm.	Steals, arrested once. Pyromaniac; decided menace.
3	f			Mother neurotic.	Not educable; in danger because of pretty face; has made mother a nervous wreck.
4	f	14	Poor; 5 in 3 rooms.	Mother immoral.	In danger of becoming immoral.
5	m				Once in Manhattan State Hospital.
6	m	12	Poor; 6 in 2 rooms.	9 children; 3 dead; parents low type.	Immoral, evil minded; brother a moral imbecile, now in Catholic Protectory.
7	m	11		Father degenerate.	Self-abuse; degenerate.
8	m	16			Incapable of manual work; stunted in infancy by wine.
9	f	11			Spine injured by fall when a baby.
10	f	13	Poor; 7 in 3 rooms.		Self-abuse; very immodest.
11	m	11	Poor		Smokes; steals; cruel; criminal tendencies.
12	m	13	Poor; 4 in 2 rooms.	10 children 5 dead; father neurotic; suicide.	Epileptic; defective vision; unable to earn living.
13	m	10	Good; 5 in 7 rooms.	Father suicide; mother insane.	Self-abuse; excitable; dangerous.
14	f	12		Child injured at birth.	Not educable; speech defective; in danger of becoming immoral.

TABLE A—*Continued*

Case	Sex	Age	Home	Family	Characteristics
15	m	12	Fair; 7 in 5 rooms.		Spinal meningitis in infancy; bad tendencies growing worse; smokes; steals; travels with rough gang.
16	m	15	Bad; 3 in 2 rooms.		Steals; easily led; incapable of self-support.
17	m	12	7 in 3 r'ms.	Father tb: mother malnutrition.	Fell down stairs when an infant. Self-abuse; cruel; suspicious; evil temper; dangerous.
18	m	10	5 in 2 r'ms.		Self-abuse; incapable of self-support.
19	m	12			Defective vision; immoral.
20	m	9	7 in 3 r'ms.		Defective speech, teeth and eyes; obstinate; a fighter; incapable of self-support.
21	f	10			Defective speech, teeth, gait; seriously ill in infancy; in Randall's Island for a time.
22	f		Bad; 3 in 4 rooms.	Mother fm; not married to present husband.	Attractive; in danger of becoming immoral.
23	f		Bad; 11 in 6 rooms.	13 children; degenerated stock.	Mongolian; incapable of self-support.
24	f	10			Custodial case; has a mania for being with boys.
25	f	15	Good		Moral imbecile; no self-control; curvature of the spine.
26	f	12	Poor; 7 in 3 rooms.		Attractive; in danger of becoming immoral; convulsions and two bad falls in infancy.
27	m	11	Bad; 9 in 3 rooms.		Defective speech, hearing, gait; tonsils, adenoids; sullen; incapable of earning living.
28	m	8	6 in 4 r'ms.		Irresponsible, incapable of earning living; defective speech, gait; very nervous.
29	m	12	8 in 3 r'ms.		Defective gait; defective palate, can't swallow; irresponsible; incapable; ape-like.

TABLE A—*Continued*

Case	Sex	Age	Home	Family	Characteristics
30	m	12	Good; 6 in 5 rooms.		Steals; lies; incapable.
31	f	11	Poor; 2 in 2 rooms.		Self-abuse; steals; lies; easily led.
32	f	15		Syphilis	Immodest; mania for being with boys.
33	f	13	Bad; 8 in 5 rooms.	Parents immoral.	Easily led; institution case; parents do not wish to lose earning power.
34	f	9	Bad; 8 in 5 rooms.	Degenerated stock.	Self-abuse; easily led; parents do not wish to lose possible earning power.
35	m	9	Fair; 7 in 5 rooms.		Brain fever; self-abuse; criminal tendencies; on Randall's Island.
36	m	16	Good; 3 in 3 rooms.		Diphtheria, convulsions, bad fall in infancy; defective eyes, gait; on Randall's Island, parents claim he was not treated well.
37	m	11	Bad.	Mother fm; father deserted; brother fm; sister has illegitimate child.	
38	m			Father fm.	Mongolian; incapable of mental or manual work; self-abuse; habitually silent; mother unkind.
39	m	14	Bad; 4 in 3 rooms.	Mother alcoholic; brother fm.	Smokes; bites nails; one eye destroyed by accident; constantly scratching it; truant; parents want earnings.
40	f	13		Brother fm; sister epileptic.	Self-abuse; untrainable; drain on family.
41	m	16	Bad; 7 in 4 rooms.	Father tb; mother delicate.	Self-abuse; bad language; truant; once created panic in school; once on Randall's Island; parents want earnings.
42	m	14	Bad.	Mother fm; brother fm; 3 brothers backward.	Irresponsible; easily influenced.

TABLE A—*Continued*

Case	Sex	Age	Home	Family	Characteristics
43	f	14		Sister abnormal.	Defective teeth, palate; very immoral; boys and men constantly after her; once in children's court.
44	m			Parents first cousins; 11 children, those living physically or mentally defective; majority were stillborn or died in infancy.	This boy is paralyzed.
45	f				Drugged in babyhood; cannot be trusted alone; abuses other children.
46	m	16	Fair		Scarlet fever; defective speech; small head; incapable; self-abuse; steals; criminal tendencies.
47	m	15	Fair	Parents cousins; family neurotic.	Hydrocephalus; paralysis; heart disease.
48	m	8	11 in 5 rooms.		Self-abuse; eleventh child.
49	m	10	Fair		Defective sight; unteachable.
50	m		Good; 3 in 5 rooms.	Mother alcoholic; 7 children, 6 dead.	Seventh child; defective eyes; self-abuse.
51	f	14			Defective eyes; immoral, two or three cents buys any privilege; sells candy in moving picture show.
52	m	14			Double set of teeth; high palate; one eye removed; high grade, might be self-supporting under direction.
53	f	8	Very bad.	Mother dead, tb.	Chorea; might improve under proper home conditions.
54	m	13	Poor; 4 in 3 rooms.		Defective speech, hearing, sight; self-abuse.

TABLE A—*Continued*

Case	Sex	Age	Home	Family	Characteristics
55	f	13		Parents drink.	Chorea, anaemia; self-abuse; immoral; incorrigible; sister the most immoral girl in the school.
56	m	14	Fair; 8 in 6 rooms.		Defective eyes, speech; grins, shuffles, falls easily; irresponsible; incapable.
57	m	15	Poor; 4 in 2 rooms.		Defective eyes; self-abuse; in a home for 3 years; neglected by mother, left alone in a tenement for a month.
58	m	10	Poor; 8 in 5 rooms.	Parents alcoholic; sister has withered arm.	Chorea; twitching of face; spinal meningitis; self-abuse.
59	m	12	Good		Very handsome; physically strong; uncontrollable; dangerous. Mother has been so good to him that he has learned nothing. Cannot button clothing.
60	m	12	Bad	Brother fm, now in Syracuse.	Adenoids, tonsils, defective eyes; steals, lies; self-abuse; often seems drugged.
61	m	15	Bad	Father fm, neurotic, cruel; father's mother the same.	Pliable, easily influenced.
62	m	12	Bad	7 children, 4 died in infancy; 3 living, fm.	Self-abuse; bad language; eats anything; like wild animal; corrupting all the little boys of the neighborhood.
63	f	7	Bad	Parents abnormal; brother fm.	Once on Randall's Island, parents objected to having her placed with custodial cases.
64	m	9	Bad	Father half-breed Indian and negro; imbecile; alcoholic; mother hallucinations; sister fm.	
65	f	13	Poor; 7 in 5 rooms.	Parents drink; 8 children, 3 dead.	Scarlet fever; operation on ears and tonsils; self-abuse; dishonest.

TABLE A—*Continued*

Case	Sex	Age	Home	Family	Characteristics
66	f	15	Bad; 5 in 3 rooms.	4 children, backward.	Children need better care and nourishment.
67	m	9	Fair	Father drinks.	Typhoid fever in childhood; docile or violent, extremes; arrested twice.
68	m	11	Poor; 9 in 3 rooms.	9 children, 2 dead; 2 dull; 1 fm.	Fell on head; can't talk so that he can be understood.
69	m	10	Fair	Parents cousins.	Cleft palate, hair lip; self-abuse; mentally a child of 3; easily influenced; at mercy of loafers.
70	m	14	Bad	Father deserted mother; mother immoral.	Slept in the streets in a box; broke arm and leg in temper fit; came to school last year with revolver; sent to Catholic Protectory.
71	f	20	Poor	Mother irresponsible.	Cretin; dwarf-like, old face; physically a woman, mentally a child of seven.
72	m	13	Good; 6 in 8 rooms.	Brother low grade imbecile; grandfather fm.	Self-abuse; not educable; dangerous if excited.
73	f	14	Poor	Family degenerate; cousin fm.	Has to work hard at home; tormented by other children. Immoral in thought and speech.
74	m	12	Fair.	Scarlet fever.	Mongolian; no co-ordination; defective speech; easily led.
75	f	10	Fair.	3 children living; 12 dead.	Mal-formed head and body; defective eyes; incapable; happy and obedient; hounded by bad boys in the street.
76	m	8	Poor.		Defective vision and gait; steals; incapable; stubborn; sly.
77	m	14	Poor; 9 in 4 rooms.		Weighs 200 pounds; may have elephantiasis; very bad odor; incapable; indolent; afraid to be on the streets.
78	m		Poor.	Father drinks; brutal to wife before boy's birth; mother abnormal.	Boy 3 years in House of Refuge for stealing; incapable.

TABLE A—*Continued*

Case	Sex	Age	Home	Family	Characteristics
79	m		Good.	Mother fm; brother in Catholic Protectory 1 year.	Strong physically; irresponsible; sixth of 6 children.
80	m				Arrested twice for stealing, suspended sentence.
81	f				Has " schnapps " for breakfast.
82	m	14		Mother insane, separated from father; father abnormal; 4 children; 1 insane, 1 fm, 1 immoral, on Island.	Speech defect; thieves; lies; violent.
83	m	13	Poor; neglected.	Sister imbecile.	Self-abuse; incapable; easily led.
84	f	12	Good; 8 in 5 rooms.		Sixth of 6 children; mongolian; pneumonia; scarlet fever; recently set house on fire carelessly.
85	f	11	Poor; 5 in 2 rooms.	Mother fm, tb, chorea; 8 children, 4 dead; 1 fm.	Neurotic.
86	m	11	Good; 5 in 6 rooms.	Father alcoholic, immoral, separated from mother.	Pyromaniac; dangerous.
87	m	11			Carefully trained by mother; withdrawn from Randall's Island.
88	m	13	Poor.	Brother fm, with same characteristics; 11 yrs. old.	Tubercular glands; truant; self-abuse; steals; immoral; runs streets.
89	m	10	Poor.	4 children; 1 backward; 3 fm.	On Randall's Island for a time; indecent habits; self-abuse; drools; injures other children; excluded from school.

TABLE A—*Continued*

Case	Sex	Age	Home	Family	Characteristics
90	f	11			In danger; has already been accosted.
91	m	14	Poor; 11 in 4 rooms.	Father fm; mother fm; brother fm, 9 years old, same characteristics.	Self-abuse; steals; lies; immoral; cruel; cowardly; quarrelsome.
92	m	14	Good; 6 in 4 rooms.	Father syphilitic; mother fm; brother same characteristics.	Self-abuse; violent temper.
93	m	7			Diphtheria; scarlet fever; badly burned; defective teeth and speech; one leg short; eats anything.
94	m	11		Parents drink.	Smokes; swears; violent temper; torments and injures other children; knocked another child from window when two years old, caused fractured skull.
95	m	14	Good.	Parents cousins.	Faulty ears; nose deflected; delicate; gentle; incapable; lovable; spits into desk or hat.
96	m	10	Fair.	Fifth of 7 children, 3 dead.	Emotional, hysterical; easily led; gets lost if he is not brought to school, only a block away from home.
97	m	11	Good.	2 children, 1 dead.	Stomach trouble; convulsions; epilepsy; dumb.
98	f	11	Good.	3 children, 2 dead.	Pressure on skull; may possibly be relieved by operation.
99	m	7	Fair.	Father drinks; father has 2 insane uncles.	Head droops; defective speech; instruments at birth injured skull.
100	f	13	Good; 3 in house.		Seems insane; defective speech; violent when angry; scratches flesh from other children.

Feeble-minded Children Formerly in Ungraded Classes

The ungraded classes have been in existence too short a time for the individuals who have had the advantage of being in them to declare themselves definitely in regard to their ultimate fate. However the after-history of eighty persons who have been in these classes indicates that much of the benefit of the training received there is lost through lack of subsequent training. In Table B is given the after-history of fifty cases selected at random. These persons are between the ages of ten and twenty; 21 of them are of Jewish parentage (Russian or Austrian), 10 of German parentage, 6 Italian, 5 Irish, 1 Swiss, 7 native. Two show signs of being able to hold permanent employment; 5 have worked steadily for a few weeks at an average wage of $3.50; 12 others have worked a few odd days; a few help with the housework at home. The majority are utterly incapable.

These persons left the ungraded class:

(1) Because of the necessity of entering some institution, penal or custodial;

(2) Because, having reached the limit of school age, they could be no longer retained;

(3) Because their parents insisted upon their going to work.

The small number of cases and the incompleteness of individual histories prevent sweeping conclusions, but the facts disclosed indicate:

(1) That such individuals are incapable of earning their living without supervision;

(2) That they are a menace to the community when unrestrained;

(3) That they are subjected to temptations which tend to lead them into a penal institution;

(4) That in an educational or industrial institution, they might lead a useful and happy life.

They further indicate that after discharge from the ungraded class individuals should be followed up by some competent authority to the end of knowing:

(1) To what extent they received lasting benefit from their training in the public schools;

(2) What is the best method of dealing with them after they leave the school; and

(3) Where the centre of infection which they represent is located.

TABLE B

FEEBLE-MINDED CHILDREN FORMERLY IN THE UNGRADED CLASSES OF THE PUBLIC SCHOOLS

FIFTY TYPICAL CASES

Case	Sex	Age	Home	Family	Characteristics
1	m	19	Poor; 10 in 4 rooms.	8 children in family; 6 abnormal.	Carrier for clothier at $5.50 a week; night school.
2	m	18		1 brother abnormal; out of employment.	Smokes; steals; lies; nothing to which he can turn his hand; peddler for a while; lost job.
3	m	17	Fair		$5.00 a week.
4	m	13	Good		Steals; very stout, once hired, for a pittance, to exhibit himself as fat boy; arrested 4 times; in reformatory since leaving school; incapable.
5	f	20	Good	1 sister, 18; fm.	Incapable; at home; does nothing.
6	m	18	Fair		Bad temper, "cranks;" roving streets; employed for a short time in soap factory, lost job; arrested once, paroled.
7	m	16	Poor		Adenoids, defective speech; shuffling gait; papers made out for Syracuse; working at pasting, $2.00.
8	m	17			Hydrocephalic; pulled threads in a tailor shop for a while.
9	m				Paralytic; on streets most of the time.
10	m	16	Bad		Tb; defective eyes; cleft palate; smokes; steals; roams streets; unable to care for himself; idiotic.
11	m		Poor		Idiot; burned to death because he was too stupid to walk away from the fire.

TABLE B—*Continued*

Case	Sex	Age	Home	Family	Characteristics
12	m	16			Easily led; can do neither mental nor physical work; transferred from Randall's Island to Syracuse, came home on vacation, overstayed time, parents will not pay for return.
13	f	17	Poor	Parents alcoholic.	Defective teeth; fond of boys; worked few weeks in factory; mother wants to place her in service.
14	f	15			Epileptic; immoral; attractive; "looking for work."
15	f	17	Poor		Housework at home for a time; ruching, six weeks, $3.50; mother would like to have her taught to work; walks the streets at night with her "lady friend."
16	m	17			Defective eyes; no co-ordination; stubborn, incapable, disobedient; arrested many times; has worked occasionally on moving vans or at painting; is usually discharged after half a day.
17	m		Poor	Brother fm; 9 children; shiftless.	Has sold papers; cannot hold job, loses it at once.
18	f	14	Poor		Ill in infancy; repulsive; was on Randall's Island, withdrawn because mother was lonely; easily led.
19	m	16			Partially paralyzed; was on Randall's Island; withdrawn to help father in saloon.
20	m	13	Poor; 3 in 1 room.	Mother alcoholic; on Blackwell's Island.	Club-footed; peg teeth; quarrelsome; has been in Catholic Protectory twice.
21	m	16	Poor	Mother fm.	Enlarged glands; bad teeth; has tantrums; steals; criminal tendencies; sometimes peddles.
22	f	18	Fair		Does housework at home; papers have been made out for Newark, parents object because of possible earning power; will probably injure someone in temper fit.

TABLE B—*Continued*

Case	Sex	Age	Home	Family	Characteristics
23	m	17		Mother fm; mother's father fm.	Incapable; run over by express wagon; sometimes runs errands or does odd jobs.
24	m	16	Fair		Scarlet fever; heart disease; rheumatism; defective vision; incapable; at home, does no work.
25	f	16	Fair		Helps with housework and care of children; once worked in saloon; "expects to marry."
26	m	18			Has been arrested; never worked.
27	m	17		Father tb.	Runs errands.
28	m	13		Sister fm, married.	Low grade idiot; self-abuse; runs streets.
29	m	11			Bad language; corrupts smaller children; violent; runs streets; incendiary tendencies.
30	m	16	Poor	Mother fm; sister deaf mute.	Has been in the House of Refuge and in the Truant School.
31	m	16	Poor	Brother fm; sister backward.	Steals; runs streets; has been arrested five times.
32	m	15			Worked a few weeks, had trouble with employer; high grade, capable of work.
33	m	16			Worked two weeks in laundry.
34	f	16			Immoral: needs constant supervision; violent temper; in candy store a few weeks filling boxes; spends evenings on the streets or bridge.
35	f	17	Fair		Epileptic; at home, incapable of doing any work.
36	m	16		Family irresponsible.	Self-abuse; papers made out for Rome, family refused at last moment; engaged to be married.
37	m	17		Parents dead; lives with sister.	Vagrant; imbecile.
38	f	17			Large, ill-shaped; pretty face; at home, incapable of doing any work.

TABLE B—*Continued*

Case	Sex	Age	Home	Family	Characteristics
39	m	18	Bad	Father tb.	Scarlet fever; odd jobs; peddling; arrested for peddling without license; in jail two days, mother paid fine.
40	m	16	Good		Defective speech; violent; at home.
41	m	18	Fair		Ricketts, palsy, paralysis; large head; incapable of work, at home.
42	m	18			Arrested May, 1909, blackmail, blackhand extortion; suspended sentence.
43	m	17			Arrested July 29 for stealing transfers; sent to Catholic Protectory.
44	f		Bad	Brother fm.	At home.
45	m	12	Bad; 9 in 3 rooms.	8 children; 1 crippled.	Eighth child; truant; smokes; runs streets.
46	m	16	Poor	Mother fm; 5 children, all fm; two sisters have illegitimate children.	Moral degenerate; smokes; cruel; vicious; delivery boy, 25 cents a day; father objected to his work; at home helping mother; various attempts made to get him committed balked by mother; called "Fire" in a moving picture show and caused panic.
47	m	16		Parents alcoholic; mother dead.	Relatives support him with difficulty; for a time in a factory; for a time peddled; cannot work steadily enough to earn living.
48	f			Parents alcoholic; mother fm; 4 members of family on Randall's Island.	On Randall's Island.
49	f	17			Quiet and good; housework at home.
50	f	10		18 children in family; 4 living.	Truant; steals; now in House of Good Counsel, White Plains.

Feeble-minded Persons Discharged from Institutions

Through carelessness, lack of interest, overcrowded conditions, or parental interference it often happens that feeble-minded individuals who are under the care of the authorities are thrown back upon the community. The dangers attendant upon such a course can not be too strongly emphasized.

Again and again feeble-minded women come pregnant to maternity hospitals and almshouses, only to leave after the birth of a child and return again in the same condition later. Again and again they are discharged "cured" from insane asylums only to return again after the birth of a child.

Under present conditions the managers of institutions for the feeble-minded are often powerless to hold serious cases that have been committed to their care because of a paternal request for discharge, even though experience shows that feeble-minded individuals who may improve under the discipline of an institution lose the benefits of the training they have received when they leave it, and again become dependent, or drift into crime or immorality.

The number of cases discharged from penal institutions to go out into the community without restriction, is appalling. Feeble-minded individuals who have already manifested a criminal tendency should at least be registered, definitely located, and supervised so that they would not eventually be placed in responsible positions such as running a passenger elevator[1] where they may endanger the physical safety of an unguarded public. To turn them adrift after their defect has been recognized seems the height of mismanagement. A proper segregation law would give to the State power to control the movements of feeble-minded persons. It would prevent improper incarceration in penal institutions and would permit commitment to a suitable institution whenever the defect is recognized.

Reginald P.

Male; 24 years old; colored. His mother's aunt is feeble-minded, his father's sister is feeble-minded, his brother is illegitimate. His

[1] See following case.

mother was extremely nervous before his birth and is irresponsible. When eleven years old the boy had a severe nervous shock which left him melancholy and depressed, and subject to illusions. He became wild and unruly and, at times, violent. Twice, at his mother's request, he was committed to the Catholic Protectory (1899 and 1900), but on his release it was found that his condition had become worse. In one of his excited periods he attacked his mother and was committed to the workhouse for six months (1905). In 1907 he was again committed for six months, but was specially discharged without serving his sentence. He was also committed in 1906 to the New York City Reformatory on Hart's Island and served six months—charge, petit larceny. He was under observation several time at the psychopathic ward of Bellevue Hospital, and was once sent to the State Hospital on Ward's Island, suffering with delusional paranoia and a lack of full mental development (July 5, 1909, to September 2, 1909). He was discharged from the hospital at the request of his previous employer and for a time ran a passenger elevator. Subsequently, he made an attempt upon his mother's life and was sent to Matteawan. (1910.)

Fritz K.

Boy of fifteen years, German parentage. His father died of tuberculosis. His mother is feeble-minded. They live in abject poverty; the mother works by the day, trying to support herself and her son. This boy is nearly blind. He was excluded from the ungraded classes because of his dangerous temper. He is brutal and uncontrollable; he fights, swears, smokes, steals, plays truant. He is immoral, guilty of self abuse, and has a very bad effect on other boys. He was arrested twice for stealing; was one year in the House of Refuge. He worked one week in a grocery store. The papers were made out for his admission to Rome, but the boy destroyed them.

Lillie D.

A female, 18 years old. She is feeble-minded and has an insane sister. She was confined in Randall's Island and was considered a custodial case, but her people insisted upon having her released. As the authorities refused to allow her to return home the case was brought up before a judge who decided with the authorities. A second attempt was made later by her people. The case was brought before a different judge in 1910. Three physicians and Mrs. Dunphy appeared before him to urge that she be retained, and the former verdict was in his hands. He heard the argument of the authorities and then ordered the girl released, saying that he "would assume the responsibility."

Robbie M.

Boy, 13 years old, feeble-minded; has had scarlet fever, diphtheria, acute rheumatism. Easily led astray. Arrested for throwing stones and fined $1. Arrested for stealing, suspended sentence; arrested for stealing, paroled.

Harry G.

Boy, 12 years old, native; feeble-minded; comfortable home. Has been arrested twice for stealing; once he was paroled, once released with suspended sentence; he is wild, bad, and has a mania for setting fires. In December, 1909, he was committed, at his father's request, to the New York Juvenile Asylum—the wrong institution for a boy of this character.

Alvin H.

Boy 16 years of age. Father's grandfather, immoral, heart disease, committed suicide; father's grandmother, tubercular, died of heart failure; father's father, insane; father's brother and brother's son, insane; father, apparently, normal. Mother, neurotic; mother's brother committed suicide; mother's two sisters, neurotic, died of cancer; mother's half-brother, insane; mother's half-brother, diabetes, died of apoplexy, attempted suicide. Boy's two sisters have heart disease and are easily infected; one brother has rupture, bronchitis, marasmus; one brother, heart disease, rheumatism, rupture; one brother, rupture, pneumonia, mentally inferior. Boy a moral imbecile, has completed seven grammar grades. He smokes, steals, is immoral and, at times, murderous. His people are wealthy and his home comfortable. He has been three times in a reformatory, but has run away each time. He is selfish and apparently without natural affection. He has been working about a cheap theatre and using the opportunity it provides for immorality.

Feeble-minded Children Withdrawn from Randall's Island

In Table C is given a statement of the reasons assigned by 43 parents for desiring to remove their children from the custody of the authorities at Randall's Island. They indicate,

(1) That there is crying need to develop Letchworth Village to its full capacity as soon as possible in order to have another institution near at hand for the reception of custodial cases;

(2) That parents are unstable in their attitude toward institution care for their afflicted children and that, both for their protection, and for the good of the child and of the community, a law giving the state proper jurisdiction over the feeble-minded is a necessity.

The facts in Table C were supplied very kindly by Miss Taber of the Visiting Committee of the State Charities Aid Association. They were gathered through visits to the homes of the children.

TABLE C

Feeble-minded Children Withdrawn from Randall's Island
Forty-three Cases

Case	Sex	Age	Personal and family characteristics	On Randall's Island	Reason assigned for withdrawal
1	f	3	Child is uncontrollable; cannot talk.	Dec. 10 to Dec. 16, 1908.	Parents could not stand child's absence.
2	f	1	Father insane, dead; mother tb, dead.	Jan. 17 to Oct. 19, 1908.	Aunt objected to having child treated as if she were fm.
3	m	9	Mother dead; child has sore eyes.	Aug. 12, 1908 to Aug. 9, 1909.	Father wanted child at home but now wishes to send him back to Randall's Island as he is married again.
4	m	12	Father dead; child has sore eyes.	April 2 to July 11, 1908.	Mother dissatisfied with treatment; boy now in Grove Street School.
5	m	10	Child is blind, deformed.	May 13 to July 25, 1908.	Parents dissatisfied, thought boy neglected and hurt by other children; sent back to Randall's Island.

TABLE C—*Continued*

Case	Sex	Age	Personal and family characteristics	On Randall's Island	Reason assigned for withdrawal
6	m	13	Child was hit with stone.	Oct. 11, 1907 to J'ly 27, 1908.	Ran away; parents charge that orderly was unkind.
7	f	16		Five months.	Improved; in Catholic boarding school for a time; now at home.
8	m	5		July 21 to Dec. 23, 1908.	Parents did not wish to have him put with defectives.
9	m	5	Child is deaf and dumb; father immoral.	May 13 to July 25, 1908.	Parents claim that he was neglected.
10	f	5	Child has meningitis; skin disease; mother epileptic, alcoholic.	May 7, 1907 to Jan. 26, 1909.	Only child, mother did not want her sent to Syracuse; will be sent back to Randall's Island.
11	m	9	Father drinks; 9 children supported by 3 oldest girls.	Oct. 9 to Oct. 30, 1908.	Parents dissatisfied because put with idiots; Syracuse too far; now in ungraded class.
12	m	18		Sept. 4, 1907 to Mar. 11, 1908.	Worked out doors; taught nothing; afterwards worked on wagon; lost his job.
13	f	8		Dec., 1908 to Jan., 1909.	Did not improve; now in Rhinelander School.
14	f	10	Child is microcephalic; father tb; charity.	Jan. 25 to Feb. 4, 1909.	Mother missed her; now in public school.
15	m	21	Picked up on street in fit and sent to R. I.	Jan. 2, 1908 to Jan. 25, 1909.	Parents did not want him sent to Rome; took him home as soon as they found him.
16	m	12		One month.	Thought him able to leave.
17	m	4	Can't talk; mother tb; brother tb; 9 children.	April 30 to July 7, 1908.	Thought him worse after contact with other fm children.
18	m	15		— to Oct., 1908.	Ran away from home; whereabouts not known.

TABLE C—*Continued*

Case	Sex	Age	Personal and family characteristics	On Randall's Island	Reason assigned for withdrawal.
19	f	5		Feb. to July, 1908.	Mother wanted her at home.
20	f	6	Epileptic.	Aug. to March, 1908.	Thought him worse after contact with other custodial cases.
21	m	10	Does not know name.	Jan. to July, 1908.	Claim that he was treated harshly; now in ungraded class, better, but learns nothing.
22	m	9	Cannot talk.	———	Mother wanted him at home.
23	f	7		— to Mar., 1908.	Objected to having him put with custodial cases.
24	f	6		Nov., 1908 to Feb., 1909.	Thought him worse after association with other custodials; in deaf and dumb institution; improved.
25	f	15		July 7 to Nov. 12, 1908.	To help mother in restaurant.
26	f	3		———	Thought her badly treated; strapped to chair.
27	m	9		— to Sept., 1908.	Better at home; grew worse when associated with other custodials.
28	f	4		July to Aug.	Mother wanted her at home.
29	m	21	Epileptic.	Sept. to Oct., 1908.	Did not want to have him with other epileptics; willing to have him sent to Rome.
30	m	33		Two months.	Keeper thought him better at home.
31	f	11		Nov. 16 to Nov. 27, 1908.	Parents missed her; now in public school.
32	f	18		Jan., 1906 to Mar., 1908.	Did not wish to have her sent to institution outside of city.
33	f	13	Epilepsy; paralysis.	———	Dissatisfied, wanted her at home, would not let her go to Craig.
34	m	6		May to Aug., 1908.	Dissatisfied; claim he was beaten by other boys.

TABLE C—*Continued*

Case	Sex	Age	Personal and family characteristics	On Randall's Island	Reason assigned for withdrawal.
35	m	9	Crippled.	June to Dec., 1908.	Has been returned to Randall's Island.
36	m	13		Feb., 1906 to Aug., 1908.	In public school for a time; then grocery clerk at $3 a week; does not work now; does not come home at night.
37	m		Sister fm.	April to Aug., 1908.	Improved; was sent home; parents will not send him back for fear of being deported; was an epileptic when admitted to the country.
38	m	10	Lame.	June, 1908 to March, 1909.	Clothes that were provided were too big; older boys imposed on him.
39	f	16	Weak back; undersized.	Three months.	Discharged at mother's request; mother boards babies and the girl tends them.
40	f	3	Paralyzed.	— to Oct. 1908 (with sister).	"Mother could not sleep while children were away;" 9 children: 1 dead, 2 fm, 3 idiots, 3 normal.
41	m	9	Mute.	Feb. to Sept., 1908.	Claimed child was ill-treated.
42	m	15	Brother epileptic.	Six months.	Mother's request; at Craig 4 or 5 years; taken away 2 or 3 times; trustees tired of readmitting him.
43	f	14	Epileptic.	Sept. to Nov., 1908.	Father could not or would not pay $2 a week.

Feeble-minded Men Paroled from Elmira

Through the courtesy of Mr. Arthur Bullard of the Prison Association of New York, I am allowed to incorporate in this report the facts in Table D.

In 1904, 450 men were paroled from Elmira Reformatory to New York City in care of the Prison Association. Mr. Bullard has obtained the history of these men before commitment to Elmira and their criminal record since they were paroled. Of the 450, 16 were declared imbecile by an examining physician, and 69 feeble-minded. Table D contains the criminal record of these defective men. Twenty-seven of them are foreign born, 40 are native but of foreign parentage, 15 are native, 2 are negroes. Of the 16 imbeciles, 12 had been arrested and 10 incarcerated before commitment to Elmira; 5 have been incarcerated since. One of the imbeciles had 6 arrests and 3 imprisonments before going to Elmira and has since disappeared. Warrant is on file against him. Of the 69 feeble-minded, 47 had been arrested and 31 incarcerated before commitment to Elmira, and 19 have been incarcerated since. In all but fourteen cases the men fulfilled the conditions of their parole and obtained their absolute release before coming again before the authorities. In cases of violated parole warrants were issued for the arrest of the men and when it was possible they were returned to Elmira to complete the term of imprisonment for which they had been originally sentenced.

TABLE D

Feeble-minded Men Paroled from Elmira

Abbreviations used in Table D: A. R., absolute release after parole; V. P., violated parole; P. P., picking pockets; L., larceny; G. L., grand larceny; P. L., petty larceny; C. C. W., carrying concealed weapons; Burg. 3, burglary third degree; At. Burg., attempted burglary; Dis. C., disorderly conduct; Disch., discharged; Fel., felonious; Sus. Char., suspicious character; Rob., robbery; Viol. P. C., violated Penal Code; R. S. G., receiving stolen goods; H. of R., House of Refuge; W. H., workhouse; Pen., Penitentiary; Tr., transferred; Ret., returned; Cath. Pro., Catholic Protectory; Juv. Asy., Juvenile Asylum.

Case	Age	Characteristics	Arrests before commitment to Elmira	Arrests after leaving Elmira in 1904
1	18	Gonorrhoea; smokes; drinks; bad associates.	PP., discharged; G. L. 2, Elmira.	PP., fined $10; PP., suspicion, discharged; PP., suspicion, discharged; PP., acquitted.
2	20	Gonorrhoea; bad associates.	C. C. W., Elmira.	
3	20	Gonorrhoea; chanchroids; syphilis.	Burg. 3, H. of R.; Burg. 2, Elmira, paroled; VP., warrant; At. Burg. 3, Elmira.	Burg. 3, Sing Sing 3 yrs.; Burg. 3, Sing Sing 4½ yrs.;
4	21	Drinks; smokes; bad associates.	Ungovernable child; Cath. Pro. twice; At. Forg., Elmira.	
5	19	Drinks; smokes; chews.	—, reformatory; Burg. 3, Elmira.	VP., warrant issued; Tramp, Pen. 30 days; ret. to Elmira; paroled; VP., warrant issued.
6	17	Bad associates; father alcoholic.	Orphan Asylum; Cath. Pro.; (mother unable to support him;) Burg. 3, Elmira.	VP., warrant issued; ret. to Elmira; term expired, discharged.
7*		Gonorrhoea; bad associates.	—Cath. Pro. 1 year; —Cath. Pro. 2 months; G. L. 1, Elmira.	VP., warrant issued; ret. to Elmira; paroled; AR.; Sus. Char., discharged.
8	20	Drinks; bad associates.	G. L. 2, Elmira.	G. L. 2, Sing Sing 2 yrs.
9	18	Smokes; chews.	Craps, fined $2; G. L. 1, Elmira.	

* Imbecile.

TABLE D—*Continued*

Case	Age	Characteristics	Arrests before commitment to Elmira	Arrests after leaving Elmira in 1904
10	21	Drinks; bad associates.	Burg. 3, Elmira.	
11	22	Gonorrhoea; alcoholic; smokes.	G. L. 1, Elmira.	
12	17	Drinks; bad associates.	—, not held; Vagrancy, H. of R.; —, paroled; G. L., discharged; G. L. 2, Elmira.	At. G. L. 2, Sing Sing 4 yrs.
13	17		Playing ball, disch.; At. G. L. 2, Elmira.	
14	18	Gonorrhoea; smokes; bad associates.	Larceny, discharged; —, jail 5 days; At. Burg. 3, Elmira.	
15		Gonorrhoea; drinks; smokes; chews; uses opium; bad associates.	Fighting, 12 days; Burg., suspended sen.; Burg. 3, Elmira.	
16	19	Drinks.	Dis. C., H. of Ref.; At. G. L., Elmira.	G. L., disch.; PP., disch.; L.; State Prison 3 yrs.; C. C. W., W. H. 30 days; Dis. C., W. H. 1 mo.; Burg., Sing Sing 4½ yrs.
17	18	Bad associates.	At. G. L., Elmira.	Now working as bricklayer.
18*	17	Drinks; smokes; bad associates.	G. L. 2, Elmira.	
19*	18	Smokes; bad associates.	Vagrancy, Hart's Island 2 mos.; G. L. 2, Elmira.	
20	20	Drinks; smokes; chews; bad associates.	Baseball, discharged; Craps, fined $3.; Burg. 3, Elmira.	VP., warrant issued; R. S. G., Elmira, paroled, AR.; —, H. of Ref. 16 mos.; Viol. P. C., discharged; Viol. P. C., fined $3; At. Burg. 2, Elmira.
21*	18		Fighting, 2 days; Fighting, 1 month; Larceny, Juv. Asy.; At. G. L. 2, Elmira.	

* Imbecile.

TABLE D—*Continued*

Case	Age	Characteristics	Arrests before commitment to Elmira	Arrests after leaving Elmira in 1904
22*	17	Bad associates.	—, Juv. Asy. 7 mos.; G. L., H. of Ref.; G. L., 2, Elmira.	At. G. L., discharged; At. G. L., discharged; P. L., King's Co. Pen. 6 mos.; P. L., N. Y. Co. Pen. 1 yr.; Vagrancy, W. H. 30 days; Dis. C., released.
23	19	Drinks; smokes; bad associates.	Sus. Char., discharged; G. L., Elmira.	Dis. C. (PP.), fined $5; Dis. C. (PP.), W. H. 10 dys.; Vagrancy (PP.), fined $10; Dis. C. (PP.), fined $5; Dis. C. (PP.), fined $10; Dis. C. (PP.), W. H. 6 mos.; Dis. C. (PP.), fined $5; Dis. C. (PP), fined $10; At. L., discharged; Dis. C., discharged; Dis. C., fined $5; Dis. C., discharged; Viol. P. C., N. Y. Co. Pen. 100 days.
24	20	Gonorrhoea; drinks; smokes; uses opium.	G. L., suspended sent.; G. L. 2, Elmira.	Now working steadily.
25	24	Gonorrhoea; drinks; smokes; bad associates.	G. L. 2, Elmira.	
26	18	Gonorrhoea; chanchroids; smokes.	G. L. 2, Elmira.	Arrested in raid on opium joint; sentence suspended.
27	23	Drinks; smokes; bad associates.	At. Burg. 3, Elmira.	Burg., —. VP., warrant issued, ret. Elmira; At. Burg. 3, Sing Sing.
28	19	Gonorrhoea; drinks; smokes; bad associates.	Stealing, susp. sentence; At. G. L., Elmira.	
29	25	Drinks; smokes.	Craps, discharged; At. G. L. 2, Elmira.	
30	18	Gonorrhoea; drinks; smokes; bad associates.	At. G. L., Elmira.	VP., warrant issued; P. L., King's Co. Pen. 1 yr.; returned Elmira, paroled; VP., returned Elmira.

* Imbecile.

TABLE D—*Continued*

Case	Age	Characteristics	Arrests before commitment to Elmira	Arrests after leaving Elmira ln 1904
31	19	Drinks; smokes.	Rob. 1, Elmira.	
32	19	Gonorrhoea; chanchroids.	Stealing, discharged; G. L. 2, Elmira.	Now working.
33	20	Gonorrhoea; chanchroids; alcoholic; smokes.	G. L. 2, Elmira.	Said to be dead, tb.
34	23	Alcoholic.	Drunk, fined $5; P. L., N. Y. Co. Pen.; Rob. 1, Elmira.	
35	27	Alcoholic.	Drunk, W. H. 3 mos.; Drunk, W. H. 3 mos.; Burg., discharged; P. L., N. Y. Co. Pen.; At. Burg. 3, Elmira.	At. Fel. assault, N. Y. Co. Pen. 1 yr.; Burg. 3, Sing Sing.
36	17	Drinks; smokes.	Vagrancy, discharged; Burg. 3, Elmira.	Enlisted in Navy.
37	18	Smokes.	Stealing, discharged; P. L., H. of Ref.; At. Burg. 3, Elmira.	
38	23	Gonorrhoea; chanchroids; drinks; smokes.	Malicious mischief, fined; Dis. C., fined; —, W. H. 5 days; R. S. G., Elmira.	Viol. P. C., Westchester Co. Pen. 3 mos.; Now working.
39	23	Chanchroids; alcoholic; smokes; chews.	—Cath. Pro. 1 year; At. G. L., Elmira.	
40	17	Chanchroids; alcoholic.	— Truant School; — Bklyn. Tr. School; Vagrancy, H. of Ref.; Vagrancy, H. of Ref.; Burg. 3, Elmira.	VP.; warrant issued; ret. Elmira; paroled; VP.; warrant, ret. Elmira; At. G. L., Sing Sing; At. Burg., Sing Sing.
41	21	Drinks; smokes.	At. G. L., Elmira.	VP., warrant issued; term expired.
42	18	Gonorrhoea; drinks; smokes.	Burg., Cath. Pro.; Burg., Cath. Pro.; P. L., discharged; Craps, 5 days; Burg. 3, Elmira.	At. Burg., Sing Sing.
43*	19	Smokes.	At. G. L., Elmira.	

* Imbecile.

TABLE D—*Continued*

Case	Age	Characteristics	Arrests before commitment to Elmira	Arrests after leaving Elmira in 1904
44	25	Drinks; smokes.	Drunk, 10 days; Assault, 30 days; P. L., 6 months; G. L. 2, Elmira.	
45	29	Gonorrhoea; alcoholic; smokes.	P. L., N. Y. Co. Pen. 6 mos.; G. L. 2, Elmira.	
46*	22	Gonorrhoea; chanchroids; drinks; chews.	P. L., H. of Ref.; P. L., jail 30 days; G. L. 2, Elmira.	VP., warrant issued; G. L. 2., King's Co. Pen. 1 yr.; Returned Elmira, suicide.
47*	16		Malicious mischief, fined $5; Forgery 3, Elmira.	VP.; warrant issued; Obtaining employment under forged name, jail 1 mo.
48	20	Gonorrhoea; drinks; smokes; chews.	At. Burg., Elmira.	P. L., King's Co. Pen. 1 mo.; L., N. J. Pen. 1 year.
49	18	Smokes.	Craps, 5 days; Susp. Per. (PP.), disch.; G. L. 2, Elmira.	G. L., Sing Sing 2 years; Now working.
50	19	Drinks; smokes; chews.	Dis. C., discharged; C. C. W., 10 days; Burg., Elmira.	VP.; warrant issued; Viol. P. C., N. Y. Co. Pen. 6 mos.; Returned Elmira, paroled; VP., warrant; G. L. 2, Elmira, paroled; AR.
51	18		Playing ball, Juv. Asy. 3 days; Craps, discharged; At. Burg., Elmira.	
52	17		Craps, Cath. Pro. 3 dys.; At. Burg. 3, Elmira.	
53	19	Smokes.	Unlawful entry, 6 mos.; Gambling, discharged; Gambling, discharged; At. G. L. 2, Elmira.	G. L. 2, Auburn 2 years.
54	18		P. L., H. of Ref.; Burg. 3, H. of Ref.; P. L., H. of Ref; At. Burg. 3, Elmira.	

* Imbecile.

TABLE D—*Continued*

Case	Age	Characteristics	Arrests before commitment to Elmira	Arrests after leaving Elmira in 1904
55	17	Smokes.	Rob. 3, Elmira.	
56	17	Alcoholic.	Rob. 3, Elmira.	—, N. Y. Co. Pen.
57	20	Drinks; smokes.	Susp. Char., disch.; Viol. P. C., 3 mos.; At. Burg. 3, Elmira.	Susp. Char., $20 or 20 dys.; released on bond.
58	16	Smokes; bad associates.	Stealing, Bklyn. Tr. Sc.; Ungovernable child; Cath Pro. 1 year; Assault, Elmira.	
59	20	Bad associates.	At. sodomy, Elmira.	
60	22	Drinks; smokes.	Assault, case dismissed; G. L., acquitted; At. Burg. 3, Elmira.	At. abduction of 15 year old girl; Sing Sing 5 yrs.
61	24	Alcoholic.	At. rape, Elmira.	
62	20	Drinks; smokes.	Burg. 3, Elmira.	
63	20	Drinks; smokes.	Orphan Asy., 5 yrs; P. L., jail, 3 mos.; G. L. 2, Elmira.	Died, tb.
64	18	Drinks; smokes.	G. L. 2, Elmira.	
65	20	Gonorrhoea; drinks; smokes; bad associates.	P. L., H. of Ref.; At. G. L. 2, Elmira.	
66	20		Peddling, fined $2; P. L., N. Y. Co. Pen. 2 mos.; At. G. L., Elmira.	P. L., N. Y. Co. Pen. 3 mos.
67*	18	Smokes; chews; bad associates.	Stealing, W. H. 10 dys.; Burg. 3, Elmira.	Now working in a moving picture show.
68	18	Smokes; bad associates.	Stealing, discharged; Burg. 3, Elmira.	
69	26	Alcoholic; smokes; bad associates.	P. L., 3 months; G. L., Elmira.	At. G. L., Sing Sing.
70*		Drinks; smokes; bad associates.	Stealing, discharged; P. L., discharged; P. L., sentence susp.; Burg. 3, Elmira.	Burg. 3, N. Y. Co. Pen. 1 year; Burg. 3, N. Y. Co. Pen. 1 year.

* Imbecile.

TABLE D—*Continued*

Case	Age	Characteristics	Arrests before commitment to Elmira	Arrests after leaving Elmira ln 1904
71*	17	Drinks; smokes; bad associates.	Breaking windows, Juv. Asy. 3 days; At. Burg. 3, Elmira.	
72*	19	Tb.; bad associates.	Gerry Soc., sev. times; G. L., discharged; G. L., discharged; Rob., discharged. Dis. C. (PP.), W. H. 2 mos.; G. L. 2, Elmira.	VP.; warrant issued.
73	26	Gonorrhoea; chanchroids; alcoholic.	Drunk, jail 1 mo.; At. G. L., Elmira.	VP., warrant issued; term expired.
74*	22	Smokes; drinks; bad associates.	P. L., H. of Ref.; Burg. 3, discharged; Burg. 3, discharged. At. Burg. 3, Elmira.	
75*	19	Smokes; drinks; bad associates.	Burg. 3, Elmira.	
76	28	Alcoholic.	Drunk, discharged; Drunk, fined $2; Arson 1, Elmira.	Now married; working.
77*	22	Alcoholic.	G. L. 2, Elmira.	
78*	16	Bad associates.	Vagrancy, —; Burg. 3, Elmira.	P. L., King's Co. Pen. 1 yr.; Assault, Sing Sing 5 yrs.
79	25	Drinks; smokes; bad associates.	Viol. game law, jail 60 days; Burg. 3, Elmira.	
80	20		Rape 2, Elmira.	Whereabouts unknown.
81			R. S. G., Elmira.	Whereabouts unknown.
82	21		G. L. 2, Elmira.	Whereabouts unknown.
83	18		Burg. 3, Elmira.	VP., warrant issued; ret. Elmira; paroled; secured AR.; whereabouts unknown.
84		Gonorrhoea.	Burg. 3, Elmira.	VP., warrant issued; term expired; unable to trace.

* Imbecile.

TABLE D—*Continued*

Case	Age	Characteristics	Arrests before commitment to Elmira	Arrests after leaving Elmira in 1904
†85		Alcoholic; habitual PP.; bad associates.	G. L., acquitted; G .L. 1, Elmira, paroled; VP., returned Elmira; tr. to Matteawan; tr. to Dannemora; ret. Elmira; "cured"; paroled; AR.	PP, discharged; Sus. Char. (PP.), 10 days; Vagrancy (PP.), W. H. 6 mos.; Vagrancy (PP.), W. H. —; Dis. C. (PP.), $3 fine; Dis. C. (PP.), $10 fine; G. L., discharged; Dis. C. (PP.), $10 fine; Dis. C. (PP.), $10 fine; Dis. C. (PP.), discharged; Dis. C. (PP.), W. H. 6 mos.; Dis. C. (PP.), discharged; Vagrancy (PP.), disch.; Vagrancy (PP.), disch.; Dis. C. (PP.), W. H.; Dis. C. (PP.), discharged; Dis. C. (PP.), $5 fine; Dis. C. (PP.), disch.; Viol. P. C., Pen. 100 days.

†Case 85 is described by the examining physician of Elmira as "A typical case of a person of inferior mentality who is a continued and heavy expense to the community."

Feeble-minded Persons Ignorant, Immoral and Prolific

Without supervision feeble-minded persons are incapable of developing their own powers and incapable of restraining their impulses, yet they are constantly held accountable for failure to reach an acceptable standard of efficiency and morality. Through poverty or punishment they pay an immediate price for existence, but the end is not there.

The ultimate cumulative burden of their criminality, of their immorality and of their defective, illegitimate children is ever growing. For this the public is paying and will continue to pay until by proper segregation, crime, immorality and increase of their kind are effectively prevented among the feeble-minded.

The facts in Table E were secured through the courtesy of Dr. Siegfried Block and of the District Superintendents of the Charity Organization Society and the United Hebrew Charities. Many of the families described are dependent upon charity for support.

TABLE E

FEEBLE-MINDED PERSONS BETWEEN THE AGES OF 7 AND 35
FORTY TYPICAL CASES

Case	Sex	Age	Home	Family	Characteristics
1	m	15	Comfortable.	Mother neurasthenic; brother sexual pervert; sister abnormal; relative insane; relative epileptic.	Tonsils, adenoids, anemic, bad eyes; steals; truant; in Disciplinary School 5 months; arrested 5 times; placed under "Big Brother's" care; found organizing theft.
2	f	19	Poor.	Mother tb.	Undersized; bad teeth; defective speech; tb.; never in school.
3	m	20		Father tb.; brother tb.; mother Fm., quarrelsome; stepfather lazy, rheumatic, intemperate.	On street, a laughing stock for children; mother would like to put him away; is prejudiced against Randall's Island.
4	f	26	Poor.		Epileptic, paralyzed on right side; has one illegitimate child; too feeble-minded to care for it; must be watched constantly to prevent a repetition.

TABLE E—*Continued*

Case	Sex	Age	Home	Family	Characteristics
5	m			Mother heart disease; sister tb.; sister paralyzed; cousin paralyzed.	Weak kidneys; uncontrolled tremors; retarded reflexes; broad palate; self-abuse.
6	f	31			Bad tempered; immoral, one illegitimate child; married twice, deserted by first husband; cared for in hospitals, and Institution of Mercy.
7	m		Very poor, helped by charity.	Father hernia, anaemia; 6 children anaemia; 4 in asylum.	Malnutrition; weak from lack of food.
8	m	12		6 children; brother imbecile; brother Fm; brother insane; sister imbecile.	Has been in House of Refuge.
9	m	14			Steals; found with a stranded theatrical troupe.
10	f	20			Cripple; illiterate; one illegitimate child; child dead.
11	m			Mother epileptic; to go to Craig; father sent to Island, nonsupport; to Elmira, burglary; to jail, desertion; killed.	Has been in Five Points Mission, Juvenile Asylum, Randall's Island.
12	m	10		11 children, 1 Fm; 2 died of diphtheria; 3 were still born; 4 died teething.	Measles, pertussis, tonsils, defective speech.
13	f	7	Very poor, charity.	Father drinks, tb.; mother's father and brother drink.	Convulsions, chorea, hysterics.
14	m	14	Comfortable.	Mother neurotic, of neurotic family; boy hates her; 4 children, 3 dead.	Handsome; ungovernable; smokes; gambles; out at night; has been in House of Refuge; found playing piano in a disorderly house for his living.
15	m	22	Poor; helped by charity.		Fm and insane; was in Central Islip Hospital, discharged as harmless.

TABLE E—*Continued*

Case	Sex	Age	Home	Family	Characteristics
16	f	17	"Spoiled by charity."	Mother neurotic; father cerebral hemorrhage; motor aphasia.	Epileptic.
17	m	18	Wealthy.	Father miserly, Fm; mother 3 times in insane hospital; suicide; brother an idiot in State Institution.	Tonsils; in Brooklyn Disciplinary School; father wouldn't pay $3 a week for keep; runs away; steals, pawns loot; head of gang of boys.
18	m	14	Poor, charity.	Father insane; mother sick from overwork.	
19	f	7	Poor, shiftless, beg; charity.	Parents drink; mother Fm.	Adenoids, bad teeth; parents improper guardians; interfere with what kindergarten is trying to do for child; pawn clothes that are given it.
20	m	22	Poor, charity.	Mother senile debility, hysteria; sister in Newark, deaf and dumb, wild.	
21	f	35			Two illegitimate children; has been in the Florence Mission, the Institute of Mercy, the N. Y. Mother's Home.
22	m	32			Syphilis; immoral; intemperate.
23	m	9		Mother syphilis.	Convulsions, epilepsy, defective eyes, large head, gait unsteady; spastic; cannot talk; can do nothing at will; no co-ordination.
24	m	15		Family neurasthenic; 7 children, twins, triplets, twins.	Tonsils, adenoids; fell on head; steals; self-abuse.
25	m	15		Mother tb.; cousin tb.; uncle tb.	Tonsils, adenoids, chorea; curses; steals; spits.
26	m	10		Father neurasthenic, immoral; father's sister insane; father's sister tb.; father's father immoral.	Adenoids, tonsils, chorea, weak heart and lungs, lame, hunchback, soft bones, weak kidneys; spits; smokes; overeats; violent; steals.

TABLE E—*Continued*

Case	Sex	Age	Home	Family	Characteristics
27	m	18			Out at night; steals; has been in House of Refuge 3 times; is easily led; caught looting a store for toughs.
28	m	14			Fell and hit head; steals; arrested 4 times.
29	f			Father alcoholic; gave child beer when a baby.	Alcoholic; immoral; insane; lived successively with 2 men; oldest child illegitimate, immoral, imbecile.
30	f	31			Immoral; 2 illegitimate children, dead; a third legitimate child, normal.
31	m			Parents alcoholic; brother crippled.	Has been on Randall's Island; now at large roving streets.
32	m	13		Father paralyzed; mother immoral; 5 children, 4 dead.	Was on Randall's Island; withdrawn because " mother wanted him."
33	f			Helped by charity.	Moral imbecile; lives with men indiscriminately; 2 legitimate children in a state institution; 3 illegitimate children, father unknown.
34	m	16		8 children, 5 sub-normal mentally; 1 physically weak; 1 physically disfigured; helped by Charities.	
35	m	21		Mother cocaine.	Syphilitic; insane.
36	f	17		Mother immoral, died in prison; father alcoholic.	In a home temporarily.
37	f				Has been in every home where mothers and children are taken; has several illegitimate children.
38	f				Insane, twice sent from Bellevue to State Hospital; twice discharged as cured; arrested, sent by Court to Waverly House, paroled for six mos.; the instant the time was up she went off on an orgy.

TABLE E—*Continued*

Case	Sex	Age	Home	Family	Characteristics
39	f				Because pregnant within a year after landing in this country, deported.
40	f				Because pregnant within a year after landing in this country, deported.

Table F—Feeble-minded Women in Bedford Reformatory

The facts in Table F were gathered by Miss Jane Day during a two months' residence in Bedford Reformatory.

Of the 300 inmates, Miss Day found 44 feeble-minded, 39 in need of permanent custodial care. Of these, 18 were the mothers of 22 illegitimate children, 3 the mothers of 3 legitimate children. All of them are illiterate, 24 are able to read and write a little, 3 are able to read but are unable to write, 8 had never been in school until they were sent to Bedford where exceedingly good instruction is furnished. Of the 44 feeble-minded, 20 are Roman Catholic, 7 Jewish, 17 Protestant; 33 spent their childhood in this country; 11 in Europe (France, Russia, Austria, Poland, Holland).

TABLE F

FEEBLE-MINDED WOMEN IN BEDFORD REFORMATORY

Case	Occupation	Charge	Character
1	Servant.	Vagrant.	One child, with mother at Bedford.
2	None.	Soliciting.	One child; has been insane.
3	Nurse-maid.	Vagrant.	One child; immoral since 14; taught children bad habits.
4	Underwear.	Associating with vicious and disorderly people.	Thinks she has been a mother, but could get no coherent statement.
5	Housework.	Vagrant.	One child in institution.
6	Housework.	Associating with vicious and disorderly people.	Two children, whereabouts unknown; can't read or write; speech defective.
7	Day's work.	Common prostitute.	Three children by different fathers, all in institutions; baby born at Bedford taken away because she taught it bad practices and could not care for it.
8	None.	Prostitute.	Suspect that she has had children; can only write "Mary."
9	Tailoring.	Prostitute.	
10	None.	Prostitute.	One child; she has 3 sisters who have each had 2 illegitimate children since she came to Bedford.

TABLE F—*Continued*

Case	Occupation	Charge	Character
11	Operator in factory.	Disorderly conduct.	
12	Errand girl.	Vagrant.	One child, negro father; says she married her mother's brother; had never been in school.
13	Operator.	Petit larceny.	Immoral at 15; father tried to ruin her; had never been in school.
14	None.	Common prostitute.	One child with her in Bedford; it appears feeble-minded.
15	Housework.	Misdemeanor.	One child badly deformed. She cannot read, write, nor tell name of aunt she lives with.
16	Waitress.	Larceny.	One child in institution.
17	Operator in factory.	Petit larceny.	One child with her in Bedford; has never been in school.
18	Housework.	Common prostitute.	One child; cannot write her name.
19	Housework.	Prostitute; suicidal; fights.	
20	Servant.	Larceny; incapable of making living.	Is now at Bedford, though term has expired; too childish to be at large; had never been in school.
21	Factory; housework.	Drunkenness; immoral since 13.	One child; knows nothing about it.
22	Housework, if any.	Grand larceny.	Has 2 children, 1 in institution; 1 she hated and gave away, loves the other.
23	Housework.	Drunkenness.	
24	Housework.	Vagrant.	
25	Operator in factory.	Moral depravity.	One child born dead owing to mother's diseased condition.
26	None.	Vagrant.	Can't be taught to read or write.
27	None.	Vagrant.	One child by her own father; immoral relations with uncle; cannot remember the time when she was not immoral; said she "likes the life so much."
28	Housework.	Abduction.	Was in State hospital 4 years; kept young girls and forced them to immoral practices.

TABLE F—*Continued*

Case	Occupation	Charge	Character
29	Bag factory.	Vagrant.	
30	None.	Vagrant.	One child at Bedford which seems feeble-minded.
31	Housework.	Vagrant.	Had never been in school.
32	Tailor.	Manslaughter.	Seduced by employer; 1 child which she has killed; suicidal; cannot read or write.
33	Cigarmaker.	Common prostitute.	Has killed 1 child; produced 3 abortions; sent to Matteawan.
34	Housework.	Vagrant.	Two children with mother; had never been in school.
35	Housework.	Disorderly.	No coherent statement about children; suspect she has some; thinks she has never been in school.
36	None.	Common prostitute.	Has attempted suicide 3 times; opium; drinks.
37	Cigarmaker.	Vagrant.	Epileptic spasms; married because doctor told her it would cure her; 1 child taken into custody when she was arrested.
38	None.	Grand larceny.	Drinks; has served so much time in institutions she can give no record of it.
39	Factory operator.	Prostitute.	
40	Housework.	Associating.	Two children; cannot read or write.
41	Housework.	Grand larceny.	One child which she killed; has been at Matteawan.
42	Housework.	Vagrant.	Drinks since 14; morphine.
43	Operator in factory.	Prostitute	One child, head deformed; it seemed feeble-minded; died at Bedford.
44	None.	Prostitute.	Two children in institutions, 1 at Bedford seems Fm.; arrested Brooklyn Navy Yard soliciting; found pregnant; sent to hospital in ambulance; child born.

Heredity Records

In order to emphasize the importance of preventing neuropathic parents from producing children, hereditary conditions in a few cases are here represented graphically. The charts illustrate the tendency of defective parents to produce defective offspring. If one parent is afflicted with feeble-mindedness, insanity, or epilepsy, especially if the taint is reinforced by Alcoholism or Tuberculosis, the probability is that one or more of the children will be feeble-minded. If both parents are neuropathic it is likely that all the children will be feeble-minded.

MINNIE H. (See p. 3.)

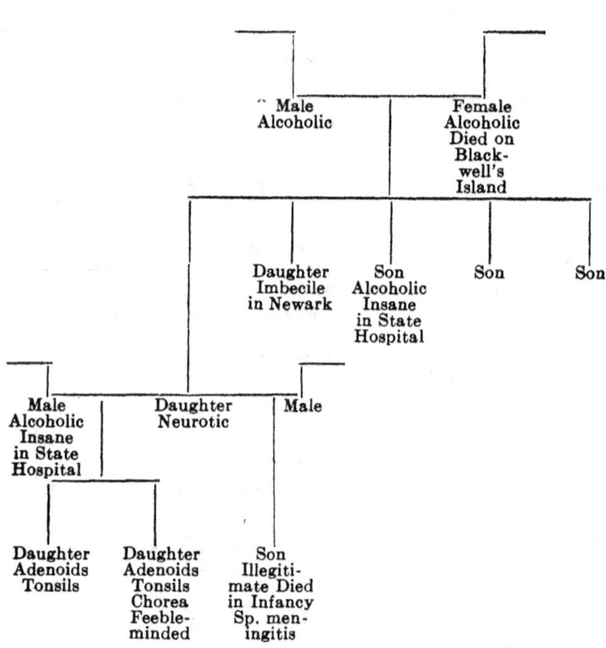

(Dependent on charity.)

Ellie R. (Hudson, N. Y.)

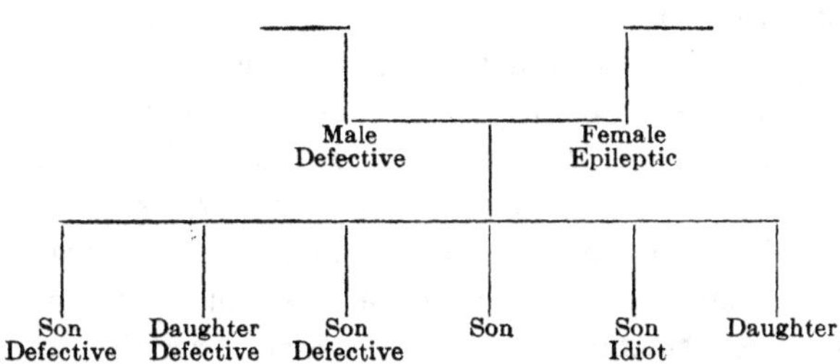

Dependent on charity. If this mother had been given custodial care when 15 the county would have been saved thousands of dollars.

Alvin H. (See p. 66.)

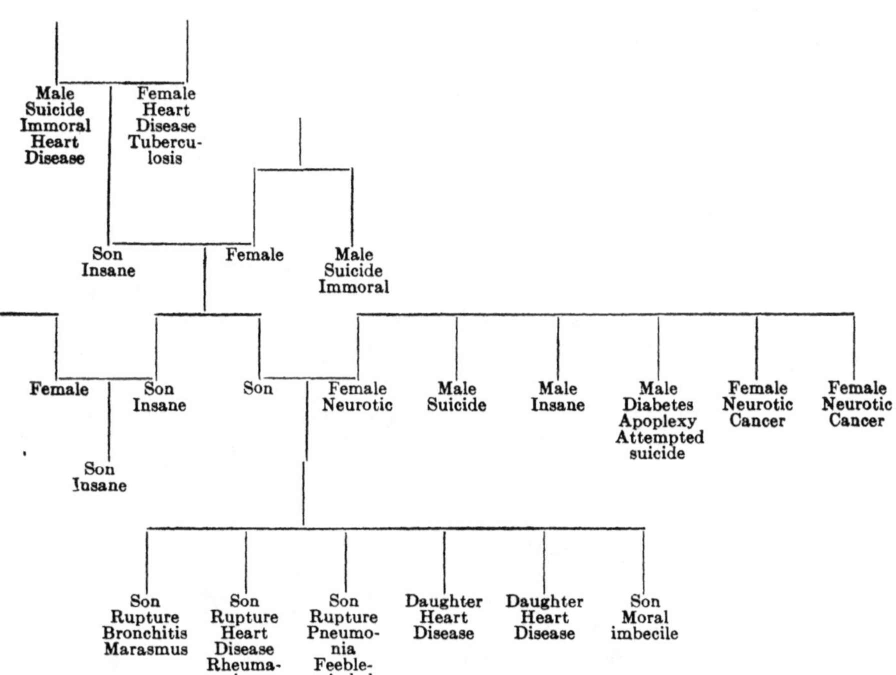

Benning Family (Cortland, N. Y.)

Four generations are still living. For generations they have been scavengers. The conditions of filth under which they have lived are almost indescribable. Recently twelve of them were found in one unventilated attic room, sleeping on two beds. They have received help from the Superintendent of the Poor for years, also from the King's Daughters and from the city. Four children are in school and the odor from their clothes makes the schoolroom almost unbearable for teachers and pupils. All the children are sub-normal; one boy helps his father as scavenger, one works out, one is a professional beggar. See following page for heredity chart.

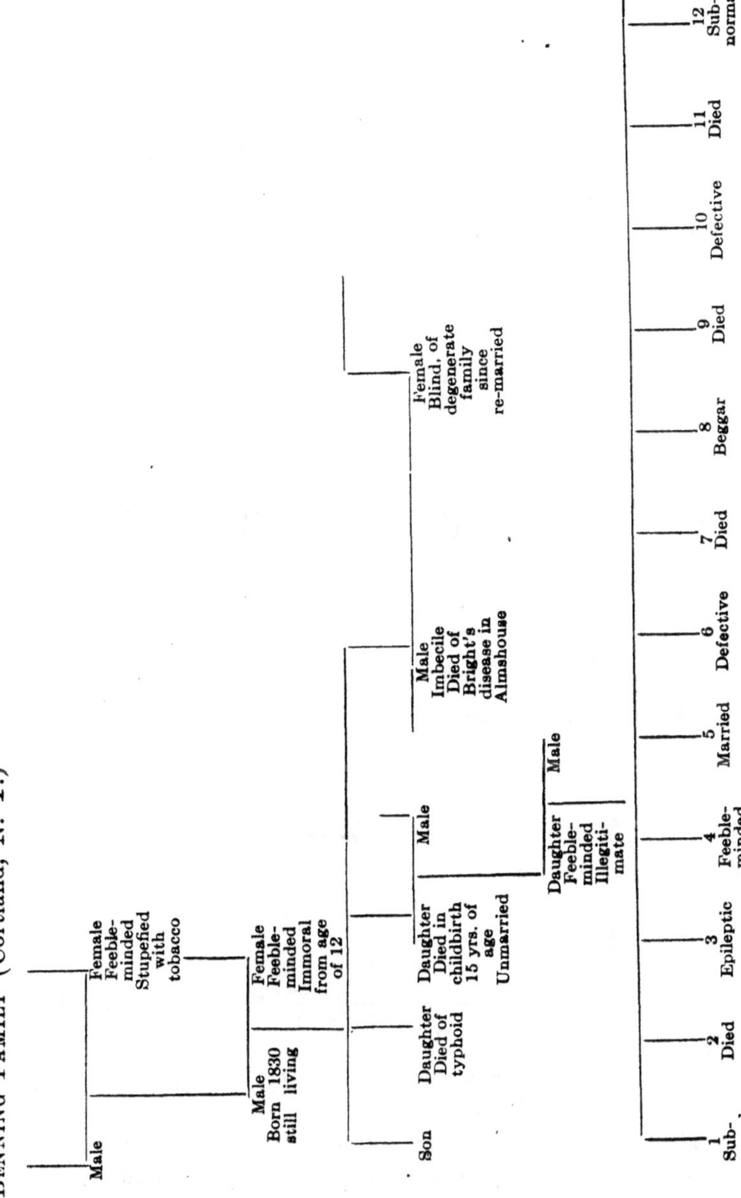
Benning Family (Cortland, N. Y.)
Male
Female Feeble-minded Stupefied with tobacco
Male Born 1830 still living
Female Feeble-minded Immoral from age of 12
Son
Daughter Died of typhoid
Daughter Died in childbirth 15 yrs. of age Unmarried
Male
Male Imbecile Died of Bright's disease in Almshouse
Female Blind, of degenerate family since re-married
Daughter Feeble-minded Illegiti-mate
Male
1 Sub-normal
2 Died
3 Epileptic
4 Feeble-minded
5 Married
6 Defective
7 Died
8 Beggar
9 Died
10 Defective
11 Died
12 Sub-normal
13 Sub-normal

SMITH FAMILY (Amsterdam, N. Y.)

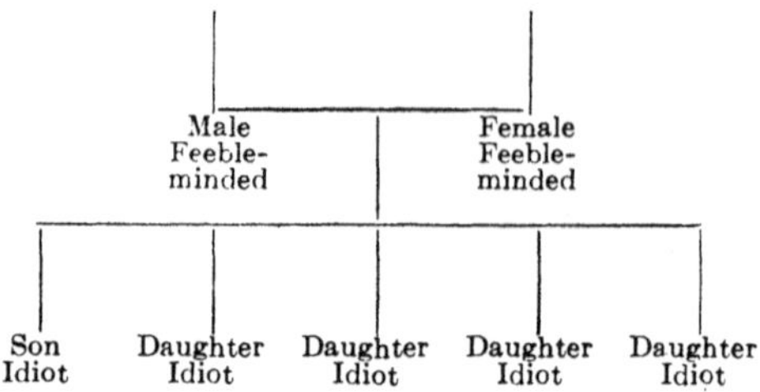

The parents will not consider placing these children in an institution because of their possible earnings.

JONES FAMILY (Hudson, N. Y.)

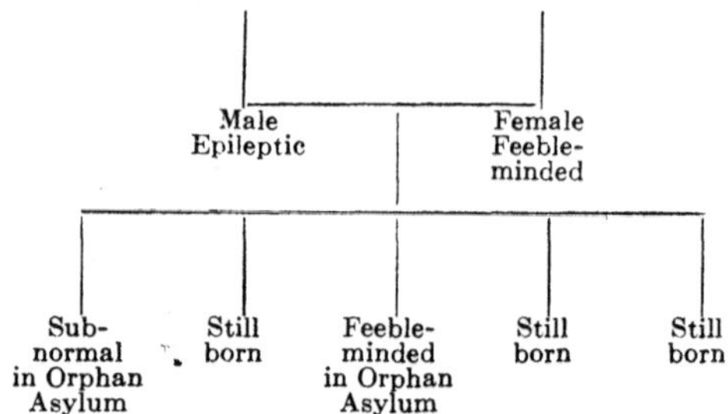

The father and mother live in a disreputable neighborhood and eat scraps furnished by the neighbors. They have a long line of degenerate ancestors, including feeble-minded, epileptics and prostitutes.

HENRY FAMILY (Newburgh, N. Y.).

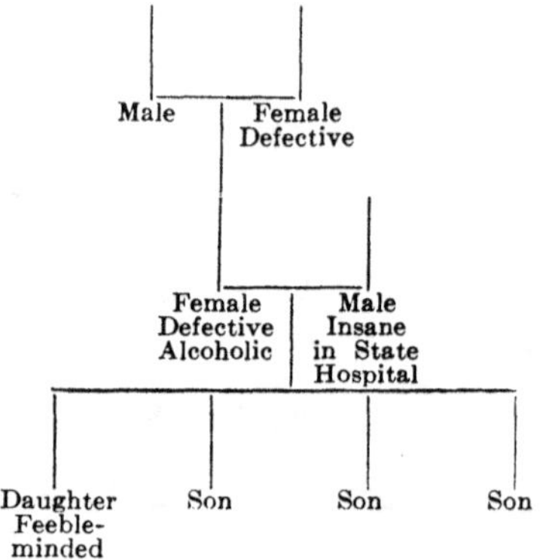

The children are in care of their defective grandmother. They were found neglected, dirty, and covered with vermin.

James Family (Hudson Co.).

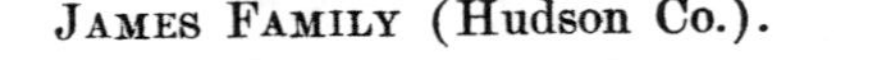

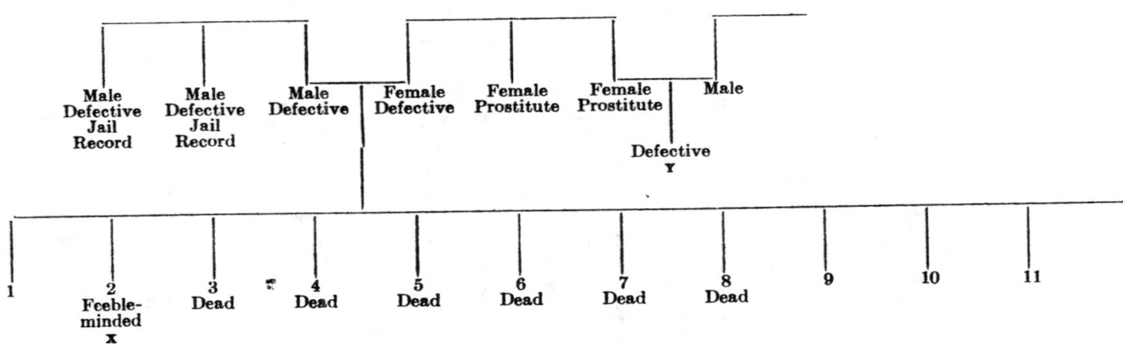

The father has had improper relations with his own feeble-minded daughter (x) and with his wife's sister's defective child (Y).

COHEN FAMILY (New York City).

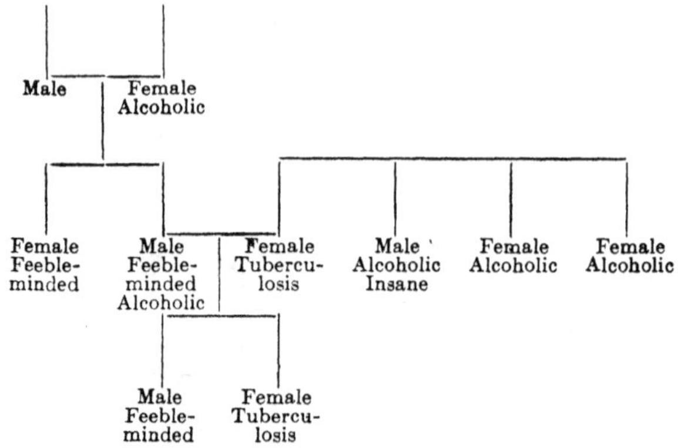

Thirteen persons live in four rooms under very bad conditions. Dependent upon charity.

MASON FAMILY (Hudson Co.).

In summer the family is self-supporting; in winter help is given by the overseer of the poor. The father and two boys can do manual work; the girls are able to work in the mills. The family will not put either the idiot son or the defective girl into an institution because of their earning power. The girls spend their free time "hanging about questionable places fooling with men."

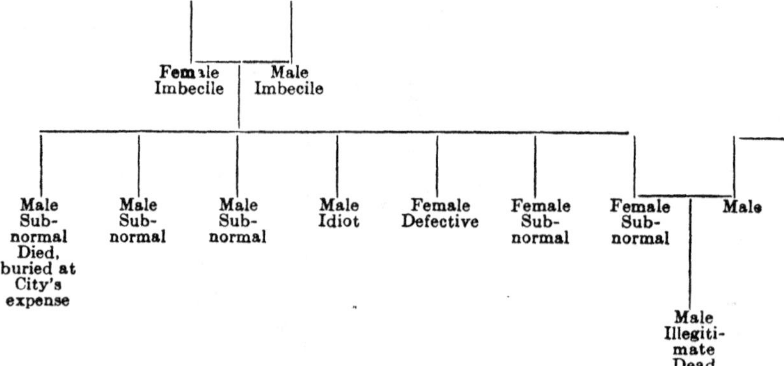

PART II

FEEBLE-MINDEDNESS AND WHAT IT MEANS

What is Meant by the Term Feeble-minded

In America the term Feeble-minded is used sometimes in a comprehensive sense to denote any degree of mental defect, sometimes in a limited sense to denote the mildest degree of mental defect. In England it is used solely in the latter sense. The general condition of mental enfeeblement is called Amentia, or Mental Deficiency; the terms Idiocy, Imbecility and Feeble-mindedness are used to distinguish the three grades of Amentia.[1]

Amentia, or mental deficiency, may be defined as "a state of mental defect from birth, or from an early age, due to incomplete cerebral development, in consequence of which the person affected is unable to perform his duties as a member of society in the position of life to which he is born."[1]

An idiot is "one so deeply defective in mind from birth or from an early age, that he is unable to guard himself from common physical dangers."[2]

An imbecile "is one who by reason of mental defect existing from birth or from an early age, is incapable of earning his own living, but is capable of guarding himself against common physical dangers."[2]

A feeble-minded person is " one who is capable of earning a living under favorable circumstances, but is incapable, from mental defect existing from birth or from an early age, a) : of competing on equal terms with his normal fellows; or b) : of managing himself or his affairs with ordinary prudence."[2]

The relation of these grades of Amentia is given in tabular form in the Appendix, page 121. Extreme cases of idiocy and imbecility are usually so clearly marked that they are easily recognized by the layman. Slight borderline cases of feeble-mindedness are often extremely difficult of diagnosis. Expert knowledge is usually necessary in these cases to determine the existence of mental deficiency. Es-

---

[1] Tredgold, A. F.: Mental Deficiency. Wm. Wood and Co., New York, 1908; pp. 2, 75, 76.

[2] Definition suggested by the Royal College of Physicians of London, and adopted by the Royal Commission, 1908, Care and Control of the Feeble-minded.

pecially is this true of that form of Amentia known as moral imbecility.

Moral imbeciles may be defined as "persons who from an early age and in spite of careful upbringing, display some mental defect coupled with strong vicious, or criminal propensities, on whom punishment has little or no deterrent effect."[1] Often such persons show remarkable ingenuity and apparent cleverness in planning their misdeeds.

The education of defective and special children under the age of sixteen is especially provided for in England. By this act feeble-minded children are defined as those "who, not being merely dull and backward, are defective, that is to say, by reason of mental defect are incapable of receiving proper benefit from the instruction in the ordinary public elementary schools, but are not incapable, by reason of such defect, of receiving benefit from instruction in such special classes and schools as are in the act mentioned."[2]

Causes Underlying Feeble-mindedness

In cases of mental deficiency the failure of the mind to attain normal development is a permanent, incurable condition due to some structural defect, or pathological condition of the brain. All causes[3] which tend to impair, or arrest, brain development are factors in the production of Feeble-mindedness. (Appendix, p. 119.) These causes fall into two classes:

1) Morbid heredity, where some ancestral, pathological condition modifies the parental germplasm before conception of the child;
2) Adverse environment, where some external factor (disease or injury) affects the embryo in the uterus, the babe at birth, or the growing child after birth.

Dr. Tredgold, who in his book on Mental Deficiency, gives perhaps the best discussion of the causes of Feeble-mindedness that has been written, estimates that 90 per cent. of all cases of mental deficiency are due to morbid heredity. In brief Dr. Tredgold's conclusions are as follows:

[1] Tredgold, A. F.; Mental Deficiency. Wm. Wood and Co., New York, 1908; pp. 2, 75, 76.

[2] Act 62 and 63 Victoria Chapter 32, Great Britain, 1899.

[3] Tredgold, A. F. Mental Deficiency, Chapter III, Causation, pp. 14-50.

Parental disease of the nervous system, especially Feeble-mindedness, Insanity, or Epilepsy, parental Alcoholism, or parental Tuberculosis, are the most frequently recurring causes. Of these causes neuropathic inheritance is the most important, for it gives rise in the offspring immediately and directly to mental deficiency. Feeble-mindedness, insanity, epilepsy in parents are responsible for probably eighty per cent. of the feeble-minded children that are born.

Alcoholism and tuberculosis are occasionally the sole and direct cause of mental deficiency, but usually when present alone their effect is remote rather than immediate. They impair the nervous system of the offspring and give rise to such diseases as migraine, hysteria, and epilepsy, which, if unchecked, culminate later, probably in the second generation, in mental deficiency. But when associated with neuropathic inheritance alcoholism and tuberculosis are most powerful contributory influences and may so strengthen a neuropathic taint as to cause feeble-mindedness in a child who might otherwise escape the taint.

Syphilis alone is not a frequent cause of feeble-mindedness because it impairs the germ cells to such an extent that it produces a high degree of sterility, miscarriages, still-born and short-lived offspring. When associated with neuropathic inheritance its virulent influence is strengthened.

About ten per cent. of all cases of mental deficiency may be traced solely and directly to adverse environment. External factors unassisted cause mental defect only when they produce a gross lesion of the brain. These factors are 1) traumatic, when injury to the brain through pressure or from a blow upon the head is severe enough to result in localized destruction of the brain tissue; or 2) toxic, when in severe cases of acute infectious diseases certain brain cells are poisoned.

Abnormal conditions of the mother during pregnancy due to disease, use of drugs or starvation, and abnormal conditions of the child due to malnutrition, disease, and other slum conditions, adenoids, enlarged tonsils, defective senses, defective teeth and defective speech are injurious to the growing child and may cause delayed development past the recovery point. They are not as a rule the sole and direct cause of mental defect. Their importance as factors in the production of feeble-mindedness lies in a powerful contributory influence when associated with neuropathic inheritance.

Number of the Feeble-minded

No census has been taken of the feeble-minded by the United States government, or by any state, which even approaches accuracy. Parents or relatives are disinclined to report one of their kin as feeble-minded; sometimes they are even ignorant that mental defect exists. As a result, the census figures are inaccurate, and the extent of the inaccuracy is not known. The nearest approximation that can be made, as to the relative proportion of feeble-minded to the whole population, is to base such estimate upon a comparatively painstaking investigation made by the English Royal Commission. This commission investigated various districts in the United Kingdom, representative of the country at large. As the result of this investigation, the commission estimated that in Scotland there was one mentally defective person to every 400 inhabitants; in England, one to every 217; and in Ireland, one to every 175. No extended investigations have been made in the United States that approximate the accuracy of that made by the English Royal Commission, and, in attempting to use the figures of the commission as applied to this country, it must be borne in mind that we are unable to determine whether or not they apply, in approximately the same proportion, to our mixed population. So far as we know, the ratio may be smaller or larger than in the United Kingdom.

The most careful work carried on in this country has been done in New Jersey, but the territory has not been sufficiently covered to obtain a complete census. However, in this state a careful test applied to a community of 10,000 persons revealed that one person out of every 200 in this community was mentally defective. On this basis, Dr. H. H. Goddard, of the Training School at Vineland, N. J., has estimated that it is reasonable to assume that there is at least one mentally defective person to every 300 inhabitants in New Jersey. Applying this ratio to New York would make approximately 30,000 feeble-minded in the state.

EDITOR'S NOTE.—The Site Commission, appointed to locate the site for the Eastern New York State Custodial Asylum, now known as Letchworth Village, after having taken into consideration the figures of the State and National census, and other data collected from institutions, estimated that there were in New York State possibly 12,300 mentally defective persons. This, it will be noted, is a wide variation from the figure obtained by using the ratio indicated above, viz.: 1 mental defective to every 300 inhabitants.

The number in institutions, or on the waiting list of institutions, in New York State, have been approximately determined as follows:

In State institutions about	4,000
In almshouses about	1,800
On waiting list of State institutions about	1,000

The indefiniteness of information regarding the total number of mentally defective persons, their location in the State, their tendency to move from locality to locality, their cost to society, their marriage relations and offspring, makes it highly important that somebody, official or unofficial, should undertake the task of securing further data.

Provision Made for the Care of the Feeble-minded

In New York State five institutions for the care of the feeble-minded have been established:

Syracuse State Institution for feeble-minded children,

Rome State Custodial Asylum for feeble-minded persons and idiots,

Newark Custodial Asylum for feeble-minded women of child-bearing age,

Craig Colony, Sonyea, for epileptics,

Letchworth Village for feeble-minded persons (in process of construction).

In addition, the Department of Public Charities, New York City, has established a Custodial Asylum and School for the Feeble-minded on Randall's Island.

Inmates are admitted to these institutions by order of the Superintendents of the Poor of the State and of the Commissioner of Charities of the cities, and upon the voluntary application of parents or guardians. They are discharged by order of the Superintendents of the Poor, or of the Commissioner of Charities, or of the State Board of Charities, or by a judge after a hearing, or by the Board of Managers of the Institution. Parents may therefore secure the discharge of their children at any time.

The weakness of the present system lies in the following facts:

(1) The capacity of the institutions is totally inadequate for the number of feeble-minded in the State. The result is that large numbers of mental defectives are at large, a menace

to themselves and to others, succumbing to poverty, disease and crime, reproducing their kind, filling the prisons, and usurping the place of the aged and feeble in the almshouses.

(2) Provision is now made only for the indigent; the great middle class who could pay a moderate sum for maintenance often do not care to take advantage of charity and cannot afford the high prices of private institutions.

(3) There is no law requiring the commitment of the feeble-minded. In many cases the ultimate decision is in the hands of parents or guardians, who are often themselves incapable of deciding what is best for the child or for the community.

Cost of Feeble-mindedness

To support a feeble-minded person in one of the state institutions costs the state, on the average, $161.20 a year. What it costs to have a feeble-minded person at large is incalculable:

(1) Primarily, because when the feeble-minded produce children they are very likely to become dependent, delinquent or diseased; these in their turn may produce off-spring of similar character.

(2) Because they cannot become self-supporting when subjected to present day competition. They are, thus, a drain upon public or private charity, or upon family strength and resources. It is impossible to estimate a cost which must include, not only the actual cost of an individual's support, but the loss sustained by his failure to be productive or by the decrease in productive power sustained by those who must use time and strength in taking care of him.

(3) Because they make up an appreciable part of the criminal class. Probably 20% (Elmira Reformatory reports 37%) of the prison and reformatory population are feeble-minded. This means, not only the expense of maintaining such persons in a wrong institution with consequent interference with the institution routine, but the expense of trial and commitment, not once, but again and again.

What this means in money may be gathered from following the evidence and procedings in any case of arson, a common crime among mental defectives.

(1) A building is set on fire with attendant danger to its dwellers, and loss of property to them and the owner.

(2) The fire department is called out. Usually six companies, involving one battalion chief, 72 men, 4 engines, and 2 trucks, the police reserves, usually about 20 men, and an insurance fire patrol wagon with an officer and ten men, respond to an alarm.

(3) The offender is arrested by a police officer, after examination of material witnesses by a fire marshal.

(4) After being taken to the station house the incendiary must go before the magistrate; and if brought to trial, with its attendant delays, much time of many different salaried officers is consumed as well as that of the material witnesses.

(5) After conviction and before sentence is passed a probation officer may be asked to look into the history of the case, which will take at least a week. The sentence may be any length of time, up to 40 years.

All this expensive machinery need not have been used in the case of feeble-minded incendiaries if they had been cared for in institutions at the proper time.

Local Studies of Feeble-mindedness

Intensive studies which have been made of specific groups of feeble-minded persons in different places reveal an unvarying condition of pauperism, degeneracy, crime and evil inheritance. The famous history of the Jukes established specifically the price that New York has paid for the degeneracy of a single family. It is estimated that this family has cost the State of New York more than has been spent for the building and maintenance of the custodial asylum at Newark, since it was first established. Other investigations indicate that it is probable that every state in the Union has some family, which after the manner of the Jukes, is preying upon its resources.

In Indiana a study of 511 families in which there were known to be feeble-minded persons yielded the following figures:[1]

Total number of persons in 511 families	1,924
Supported in public institutions	1,334

[1] Reported by Amos W. Butler, Science, Sept. 20, 1900, Vol. XIV, No. 351, N. S.

Feeble-minded	1,249
Insane	54
Otherwise defective	44
Normal, or defectiveness unknown	577
Illegitimate	267
One or both parents defective, 54% of whole number	1,024
Feeble-minded women with illegitimate children, 22% of women	163
These 163 mothers had each from one to eight children, in all	248

In a study of 803 families it was shown that in the second generation 517 individuals or 70.4% were feeble-minded.

In a study of the histories of five women it was found that they were the mothers of 19 children of whom 15 are in institutions. The time they have spent there represents a total of 136 years at $100 a year, amounting to $13,600. If the mothers had been put into custody 15 years ago the total would have been $7,500. There would not only have been a saving of money but of suffering and degeneracy.

In order to arrive at accurate knowledge regarding the causes of feeble-mindedness and its prevention, and the bearing it has on various problems of sociology, a systematic knowledge of large numbers of cases extending over a long period of time is necessary. To make available the enormous amount of material now going to waste in hospitals, schools, jails, churches, etc., some central recording agency is necessary.

In the office of the Board of State Charities of Indiana such an agency has been established. It is at present of great value to the officers of charitable institutions, who avail themselves of its help in determining the disposition of cases that come before them. It will be of untold value to future students of sociological problems, because of the mass of well arranged material that is being gathered together. Regular reports are sent from all institutions monthly or quarterly, giving salient facts regarding the individual and family history of each inmate: name, age, sex, color, nationality, mental and physical condition, whether legitimate or illegitimate; names and specific information regarding parents, whether affected with insanity, feeble-mindedness, deafness, blindness, paralysis, whether pauper, criminal, or drunkard, etc. This information is transferred to cards that are properly filed and available for instant use. Every fragment of information is added as it is received. The state at least knows what it is helping to perpetuate when it is lax in its care of individuals with bad inheritance.

The school for the feeble-minded at Vineland, N. J., is also preserving most valuable material that will be, and already is, of infinitely more value than the cost of securing it. Its heredity charts are laying the foundations for definite scientific knowledge regarding feeble-mindedness. The people who have inaugurated these systems realize that now is the time to gather material for use in the future. The longer it is put off the more valuable information is hopelessly lost.

In New York State a real opportunity is slipping away. No adequate provision has been made for preserving records, and material has been lost simply because it has not been properly classified. Many men who would be glad, because of their scientific or personal interest, to keep records, are too busy with the routine work of their positions to attend to a phase which seems unimportant when compared with an immediate pressing need. In many of our institutions, however, not sufficient care has been given to the filing of records or the securing of available information. Particularly is this true of Randall's Island. It is practically impossible to obtain adequate information regarding the history of any specific case in the asylum there, because in the record book nothing appears beyond the date of entrance and discharge, and the person to whom discharge is made. This entails a loss that will soon be incalculable.

The Royal Commission

In 1904 a Royal Commission was appointed in England to consider existing methods of dealing with mental defectives and to make recommendations for more efficient methods. The importance of the work of this Commission can hardly be over-estimated, for it represented the first systematic attempt to obtain reliable data regarding the number and condition of the feeble-minded. As no reliable statistics were available medical inspectors were appointed in various districts to visit personally all public elementary schools, poor law institutions, charitable establishments, training homes, reformatories, common lodging houses, prisons, idiot asylums, hospitals and all establishments and all individuals from whom information concerning the mentally deficient might be obtained. The results of this investigation are incorporated in the report of the Commission on the Care and Control of the Feeble-minded published in eight volumes in 1908. In this report

(1) The various grades of mental deficiency are defined and classified;
(2) The lifelong and incurable character of mental deficiency, and its spontaneous and inherited nature are emphasized;
(3) The probable proportion of mentally defective persons is established;
(4) Both natality and mortality among defectives are shown to be great. Mentally deficient parents tend to have large numbers of children and large numbers of them survive in spite of a high death rate;
(5) Mental deficiency is shown to be closely related to crime. It is estimated that 10.28% of all prisoners are mentally defective, but this is believed to be an underestimate.
(6) Alcoholism is shown to be closely related to mental defect. It was found that 62.7% of all chronic inebriates are mentally defective, and that mentally defective persons react to the effects of alcohol more readily than do normal persons.
(7) Mental defect is shown to be closely related to illegitimacy. Feeble-minded women give birth to a large number of illegitimate children and these children tend to inherit the defect.
(8) The present methods of dealing with mental defectives through the Lunacy Commission, the Poor Law Guardians, and the Educational authority in England are described.

The Lunacy Commission and the Poor Law Guardians have permissive powers to care for feeble-minded persons upon recommendation of a qualified practitioner, but provision is inadequate in asylums and persons are maintained rather than treated in almshouses.

In accordance with the Elementary Education Act of 1899 a local educational authority may, with the approval of the Board of Education, make arrangements for ascertaining what children in its area are defective and epileptic and make provision for the education of such children,

(1) By establishing classes in public elementary schools certified by the Board of Education as special classes, or
(2) By boarding out, subject to the regulation of the Board of Education, any such children in a house conveniently near to a certified special class or school, or
(3) By establishing schools certified by the Board of Education for defective children.

The expense is borne by the local educational authority, though the state makes a grant to schools conducted in accordance with the act. Each child costs in a day school £10, in a residential school £30.

Though this act is permissive and not obligatory, London and twenty of the largest towns have adopted it. The system is better than ours because, while the establishment of schools and classes is left to the discretion of the educational authority, parents must cause a defective or epileptic child to attend school, if a school is within reach of its residence, until it reaches the age of sixteen. As poor law schools have government permission to extend the age limit to twenty-one years, it is in many cases possible to gain control over the feeble-minded for life.

The system is not, however, entirely effective, for it has been found in England, as it has been found here, that the effects of training in special classes are not lasting without subsequent supervision. The after-care sub-committee of the city of Birmingham established an employment bureau, and during a period of nine years studied the history of 650 mentally defective children who had passed through the special classes. The employment bureau was finally given up, for it was found that only the highest grade of mental defectives could obtain or retain positions. At least 65 per cent. failed to secure remunerative employment; fifty-seven earned as a weekly average 6s. 1d.

This sub-committee endorsed the opinion previously expressed, that for a large percentage of the feeble-minded supervision is necessary,

(1) To enable them to contribute to their own support;
(2) To save them from vicious habits;
(3) To save them from harsh treatment at home and on the street;
(4) To prevent their becoming drunkards, criminals and prostitutes;
(5) To prevent their giving birth to children who can only grow up to be a burden to the community.

When once permanent care is enforced, the schools and special classes will be a valuable part of the scheme because by registering all the children in a district and emphasizing the need for special care they will serve as a connecting link with institutions.

(9) The Royal Commission recommends that as legal powers of detention are at present insufficient, State care be provided for all feeble-minded persons. It suggests that the following principles should govern state care of the feeble-minded:

(1) Persons who cannot take a part in the struggle of life owing to mental defect, whether they are described as lunatics, or persons of unsound mind, idiots, imbeciles, feeble-minded or otherwise, should be afforded by the state such special protection as may be suited to their needs.
(2) The mental condition of these persons and neither their poverty, nor their crime, is the real ground of their claim for help from the state.

(3) If mental defectives are to be properly considered and protected as such, it is necessary to ascertain who they are, and where they are, and to bring them into relation with the local authority.

(4) The protection of the mentally defective person, whatever form it takes, should be continued as long as it is necessary for his good. This is desirable not only in his interest but also in the interest of the community. It follows that the state should have authority to segregate and to detain mentally defective persons under proper conditions and limitations, and on their behalf to compel the payment of contributions from relations who are able to pay for their support; or should itself provide such care and accommodation as may be necessary either directly or through the local authority.

(5) In order to supervise local administration of this nature a central authority is indispensable.

(6) In regard to the protection of property all mentally defective persons should have like privileges.

(7) It is essential that there should be the closest co-operation between judicial and administrative authorities.

Conclusion

The facts set forth in this study are in harmony with the findings of the Royal Commission, and with all local investigations of the feeble-minded, made in this country.

(1) They illustrate the inability of the feeble-minded to conform to the laws that govern normal people and to hold themselves to acceptable standards of work and morality.

(2) They show that the inability of the feeble-minded to assume the responsibility for their own lives renders them a burden to their families and a menace to the public upon whom the burden of their maintenance, of their criminality, of their weakness and of their immorality ultimately falls.

(3) They indicate that feeble-minded persons respond to training and that under supervision in many cases they become self-supporting, useful individuals.

(4) They warrant the belief that by the application of vigorous measures the conditions producing feeble-mindedness may be in great measure controlled. The number of the feeble-minded may be reduced to those arising from external, or accidental causes if persons afflicted with neuropathic inheritance are prevented from having children. This preventable source is responsible at present for about 80% of feeble-mindedness.

The State has accepted responsibility for the feeble-minded by establishing institutions for their care and training. The time has come when it must for its own sake and the sake of the next generation worthily discharge this responsibility. Three things are necessary:

(1) Adequate provision for the feeble-minded in institutions designed for their education and welfare;
(2) A proper segregation law, involving separation of the sexes, which will prevent propagation of their kind, and ill-advised contact with the world at large;
(3) A marriage law which will require a clean bill of health and evidence of normal mind before a license is issued.

That the segregation of defectives costs money is remembered, that it saves money is often forgotten. The initial cost of segregation would be great but the saving effected by correcting our present lax methods would be greater. As tax bills are not itemized the ordinary citizen does not realize that he is at present paying for the unrestrained presence of the feeble-minded. An added tax for their segregation would be an apparent rather than a real increase, for through segregation of defectives, the number of criminals, the number of prisoners, the cost of trials, the demand upon public and private charity would be decreased; and as control of hereditary conditions resulted in decrease in the number of defectives, and training rendered many of them self-supporting, the expenditure necessary for their maintenance would from year to year grow less. The feeble-minded at large are as dangerous, if not more dangerous, than persons suffering from contagious disease. No consideration of cost, of parental affection and responsibility, or of personal liberty should be allowed to weigh against public safety.

APPENDIX

EDUCATIONAL CLASSIFICATION OF THE FEEBLE-MINDED

By Martin W. Barr, M. D.

(Mental Defectives, p. 90)

Idiot

Training	Grade	Type	Prognosis
Asylum care.....	Profound..	Apathetic Excitable	Unimprovable.
	Superficial.	Apathetic Excitable	Improvable in self help only.

Idio-Imbecile

(Asylum care)

- Improvable in self help and helpfulness.
- Trainable in very limited degree to assist others.

Moral Imbecile

Custodial life and perpetual guardianship......

- Mentally and morally deficient.
- Low Grade:—trainable in industrial occupations; temperament bestial.
- Middle Grade:—trainable in industrial and manual occupations; a plotter of mischief.
- High Grade:—trainable in manual and intellectual arts; with a genius for evil.

Imbecile

Long apprenticeship and colony life under protection........

- Mentally deficient.
- Low Grade:—trainable in industrial and simplest manual occupations.
- Middle Grade:—trainable in manual arts and simplest mental acquirements.
- High Grade:—trainable in manual and intellectual arts.

Backward or Mentally Feeble

Trained for a place in the world...

- Mental processes normal, but slow and requiring special training and environment to prevent deterioration; defect imminent under slightest provocation, such as excitement, over-stimulation or illness.

TABULATION OF THE CAUSES OF FEEBLE-MINDEDNESS *

I

- Inherited factors affecting the parental germ plasm before conception of the child
  - Transmitted disease of the nervous system giving neuropathic inheritance. (Causes 80% of all cases.)
    - Mental deficiency.
    - Insanity.
    - Epilepsy.
    - (Hysteria, neurosis, paralysis, cerebral hemorrhages.)
  - Vitiating disease or habits. (Causes 10% of all cases.)
    - Alcoholism.
    - Tuberculosis.
    - Syphilis.
    - Other debilitating disease.[2]
  - Sociological factors
    - Ages of parents.[2]
    - Consanguinity of parents.[2]

II

- Environmental factors[1] affecting the child
  - Before birth
    - Abnormal condition of mother during pregnancy
      - Mental shock and stress.
      - Physical injury.
      - Disease.
        - Alcoholism
        - Tuberculosis.
        - Syphilis.
        - Drugs and other poisons.
      - Age.
    - Abnormal condition of foetus
      - Injury, disease, especially of the brain.
  - During birth
    - Abnormalities of labor, such as prolongation with resulting congestion or brain extravasation of blood.
    - Convulsions or injury at birth.
    - Primogeniture.[2]
    - Premature birth.[2]
  - After birth.
    - Cretinism, or deficiency of the thyroid gland.
    - Epilepsy and convulsions.
    - Injury.
    - Sense deprivation.
    - Infectious fevers.
    - Brain disease.
      - Meningitis.
      - Syphilis.
      - Tumor or abscess.
      - Sunstroke.
    - Mental shock.
    - Malnutrition.

---

*Lapage, C. P., Feeble-mindedness in Children of School Age, 1911, pp. 203, 218.

[1]A cause of feeble-mindedness only when a gross lesion of the brain is produced, directly responsible in possibly 10% of all cases. Influence as a rule merely contributory.

[2] Of little importance unless associated with neuropathic inheritance.

CHARITY RECORD—MINNIE H (see p. 3)

1901

April 1. Visited. Furniture pawned, three months' rent ($7) due. Neighbors and relatives supplying food. Husband, previously insane, at home from Ward's Island.

April 2. Letters written and received.

April 3. Letters written and received. Woman calls at office. Friends and relatives visited. Husband intemperate. Once tried to commit suicide. Woman advised to send husband to Ward's Island and go to a home.

April 5. Letters filed.[1] Visited. They had moved, relatives providing expenses.

April 6. Letter filed.

April 8. Case considered by committee.

April 24. Visited. Friends are providing food. Woman warned that husband may do injury and that future children may be insane or epileptic.

May 6. Visitor reports that woman works, husband does not. Committee decides that case be left to relatives.

May 7. Report filed.

Aug. 19. Woman calls at office, asks for work. Reports that husband is again on Ward's Island insane.

Aug. 20. Visited. Groceries given, $1.11.

Aug. 28. Visited.

Sept. 1. Report filed.

Sept. 3. Woman calls and asks help.

Sept. 4. Visited; given $.95.

Sept. 5. Report filed.

Sept. 6. Report filed.

Sept. 7. Report filed.

Sept. 9. Committee considers case.

Sept. 10. Woman writes asking aid.

Sept. 11. Visited.

Sept. 17. Visited. Woman earns $5 a week as cleaner in a theatre.

Sept. 26. Visited. Father, mother and imbecile sister have come to live with her. Father idle.

Oct. 11. Visited. Asked to call.

Oct. 21. Visited.

Oct. 24. Visited. Woman calls. Another sister living with her. Father works odd days. Given warm clothing.

Nov. 4. Visited.

Nov. 21. Visited.

Nov. 26. Woman called. Parents in house next door, cared for by brother. Children in day nursery. Asks for clothing.

---

[1] The word filed is used for convenience and brevity. It refers not merely to the final act of storing away the letter but as well to its dictation and typing, which often involve much time and energy.

1991

Nov. 27. Thanksgiving dinner provided.

Dec. 6. Effort made to get woman to move.

Dec. 16. Letter filed.

Dec. 23. Woman asked to call for Christmas treat.

Dec. 24. Woman calls. Given $1.50, groceries, $.50, two dolls.

1902

Jan. 2. Visited. Children now left with mother instead of at nursery. Mother drinks hard.

Jan. 24. Visited. Children in nursery.

Feb. 1. Visited.

Feb. 21. Visited.

Mar. 5. Visited.

Mar. 17. Letter written to woman.

Mar. 28. Letter received from woman.

April 1. Sister Mary of —— asked to call in regard to imbecile sister.

April 5. Sister Mary reports that the priest is supervising the case.

April 23. Visited. One child with woman's intemperate mother.

May 8. Visited. Urged to keep children in nursery. Imbecile sister gone.

June 4. Visited. Woman works in boarding house, takes youngest child with her.

June 13. Visited. Case left under Sister Mary's care.

June 14. Case filed.

Aug. 4. Woman writes.

Aug. 6. Woman calls asking assistance.

Aug. 7. Woman calls asking to have home found for children.

Aug. 9. Visited. Children usually on streets.

Aug. 13. Report to Bureau of Dependent Children.

Sept. 2. Visited. Children in institution. Mother pays $1 a week for Mary, city pays for the other.

Sept. 8. Visited.

Sept. 12. Visitor reports. Woman earns $3 a week as domestic—hours 7 A. M. to 9 P. M.

Sept. 17. Visited.

Sept. 22. Case closed and filed.

Oct. 10. Mother takes children home as she has secured work again as cleaner in theatre at $7 a week.

Oct. 17. Visited. Children at home in grandmother's care.

Oct. 20. Committee considered case. Inquiry made of Bureau of Dependent Children concerning discharge.

Oct. 22. Inquiry answered.

Oct. 27. Report to Bureau of Dependent Children of conditions.

Oct. 30. Report to B. D. C.

Nov. 24. Case closed.

1903

Feb. 1. Case re-opened.

Feb. 9. Woman calls. Sick, out of work, asks aid. Given $.50.

1903

Feb. 10. Visited. Given medicine, $.30.

Feb. 13. Visited. Given $1.02. Woman calls, asks for work. Given $.25 and sent to employment bureau.

Feb. 20. Visited. House disorderly. Asks work.

Feb. 25. Visited. Asks work. Rent, $11, due, no money.

Feb. 26. Visited. Asks work.

Feb. 27. Woman calls. Given $5 and clothing. Report filed.

Feb. 28. Three days weekly work secured for her.

Mar. 10. Visited. Work provided.

Mar. 16. Visited. Children not at nursery. Neglected. Vermin.

Mar. 19. Woman calls, baby sick.

Mar. 27. Woman calls. Given clothes. Work provided.

April 6. Visited. Woman sick, declines to have doctor. Home filthy.

April 13. Visited. Advised to go to dispensary.

April 16. Woman calls. Acknowledges that she is pregnant, as result of illicit relations. Feels disgraced.

April 23. Visited. Woman sick.

April 30. Woman calls. Card to physician given.

May 11. Visited. Woman ill. Letter written to the man. N. Y. Infant Asylum visited and arrangements made to receive the woman. Woman notified.

May 12. Woman calls. Committee considers case.

May 13. Records filed. Letter from man. Woman visited. Given $1.

May 15. Letter from man filed. Woman visited.

May 16. Man seen. Promises $25 toward expenses.

May 18. Telephoned N. Y. Infant Asylum. Visited Grace Settlement and made arrangements for the reception of younger child. Made arrangements for storing furniture. Given $1.

May 19. Visited storage warehouse.

May 20. Woman calls. Several institutions communicated with. Arrangements made for reception of older child.

May 21. Notified Bureau of Dependent Children of arrangements.

May 25. Letter written to B. D. C.

May 27. $1.34 given for expenses.

May 28. Infant Asylum visited. Woman feels disgrace, fretting.

June 21. Two children visited. The younger child is taken from Grace Settlement to mother.

June 25. Infant Asylum visited. Woman confined with boy.

July 8. Older child visited. Has been taken to the country for two weeks.

July 9. Letter filed from woman. Infant Asylum visited. Woman doing well, baby not strong either physically or mentally. Younger child fairly well. Woman to remain until baby is placed by adoption.

July 13. Letter to woman. Letter to Central Islip regarding husband.

July 16. Letter from Central Islip filed.

July 31. Letter from woman filed. Letter to woman filed.

1903

Aug. 3. Letter from woman filed. Letter to woman filed.

Aug. 12. Infant Asylum visited. Woman dissatisfied with food. She wants to leave. Superintendent reports that woman, though well-intentioned, is weak morally, not able to take proper care of herself. Hesitates to recommend child for adoption.

Aug. 14. Letter to woman. 25 cents carfare given.

Aug. 17. Letter to woman filed.

Aug. 28. Letter to woman filed.

Sept. 1. Letter from woman filed. Receipt sent for money received.

Sept. 2. Visited Infant Asylum. 50 cents carfare given woman. Asks for skirt.

Sept. 3. Skirt, $2.45, purchased and sent her.

Sept. 4. Letter from woman filed.

Sept. 17. Visited Infant Asylum.

Oct. 5. Letter from woman filed. Infant Asylum visited. Woman now paid $3 a month for her services. Given $1. Woman and baby in good health. Wishes to become self-supporting.

Oct. 27. Visited Infant Asylum. Woman needs clothing.

Oct. 30. Letter from woman filed.

Nov. 13. Letter from woman filed. Answer filed.

Nov. 18. Home found for baby, but mother wants to keep it.

Dec. 7. Committee decides that mother shall keep child. Supervision to be exercised to see that father does not again gain influence over mother.

Dec. 8. Visited Infant Asylum.

1904

Jan. 2. Bill received for storage, $18.

Jan. 5. Visited asylum. Woman well, children delicate.

Jan. 11. Brother of woman calls and says mother is dying.

Jan. 13. Letter from woman filed.

Jan. 14. Visited home of brother. The father lives with him. The mother died in October on Blackwell's Island. Intemperate. Bill for storage paid, $18.

Jan. 16. Letter from Central Islip filed.

Jan. 18. Visited Infant Asylum. Conditions unchanged.

Feb. 10. Letter from woman filed. Answer filed.

Feb. 13. Two letters from woman filed. Answer filed.

Feb. 17. Letter from woman filed. Answer filed.

Feb. 18. Committee sends representative to Infant Asylum to discuss future of woman.

Feb. 19. Letter from woman filed.

Feb. 20. Report from asylum that woman works well under supervision, but has no moral strength.

Mar. 1. Discussed with member of woman's church the possibility of the woman's securing a divorce from her insane husband and marrying the father of her last child.

1904

Mar. 18. Effort made to see priest.

April 6. Effort made to see priest.

April 9. Priest refuses to sanction divorce. Promises to see after her spiritual welfare and keep the man away.

April 14. Visited Infant Asylum. Reported priest's verdict to woman.

April 22. Baby died of spinal meningitis. Request made for funeral expenses.

April 23. Visited Infant Asylum. Woman grieves for baby, but decides to let hospital bury it.

April 26. Committee considers case. Thinks woman should establish home for her two children. Has money in hand for the purpose.

April 28. Letter from woman filed. Answer filed.

May 4. Letter from woman filed and answered.

June 6. Letter to superintendent of Infant Asylum filed.

June 9. Letter from superintendent of Infant Asylum filed.

June 11. Bill for expressing package to woman, 25c.

June 14. Called at express office, paid bill.

July 1. Bill for storage, $12, asked to delay 3 months.

July 5. Letter from storage warehouse filed.

Aug. 25. Woman calls.

Aug. 30. Letter from woman filed. Friendly visitor ready to take case when home is established.

Aug. 31. Letter from woman filed. Answer filed.

Sept. 2. Secretary calls to discuss case. No action taken as youngest child is sick.

Sept. 19. Letter from woman filed.

Sept. 20. Representative of committee calls at Infant Asylum to discuss plans.

Sept. 27. Woman calls. Younger child is sick in hospital; woman earns $5 a month. Wants to make home for herself. Urged to stay at asylum till child gets well.

Sept. 29. Storage bill investigated. Letter written to woman telling her that $23.34 has been spent of the $25.

Oct. 3. Letter from woman filed. Consulted. Secretary advises that furniture be sold for storage. Tried to dispose of furniture.

Oct. 10. Effort to dispose of furniture unsuccessful, storage company interviewed.

Oct. 11. Storage company agrees to keep furniture 3 months free, if bill for $18 is paid. This bill will be paid.

Oct. 12. Consulted cashier.

Oct. 25. Woman's father calls. Wishes to find whereabouts of daughter. Has been drinking, fell on banana peel and was in hospital 15 months. Younger son insane, as result of drink and cigarettes; Manhattan State Hospital. Imbecile daughter in Newark.

Oct. 26. Letter to woman. Woman calls. Does not want to see father. Insane husband ill with typhoid fever. Younger child still ill on North Brothers Island with scarlet fever.

1904

Oct. 31. Letter from State Hospital filed.

Nov. 1. Letter from Department of Health filed. Woman's brother visited. Letter to woman filed.

Nov. 3. Letter from woman filed.

Nov. 7. Letter written and filed. Woman's father calls.

Nov. 16. Visited older child in industrial school.

Dec. 14. Letter from woman filed.

Dec. 15. Letter to woman filed.

Dec. 19. Letter to woman's brother filed.

Dec. 20. Sister-in-law calls. Committee decides to close case.

Dec. 22. Records filed.

1905

Jan. 31. Employment bureau asks information.

Oct. 20. Case re-opened. Woman has not been to see older child for two months. Called to see child.

Oct. 21. Letter to Brooklyn Bureau about woman.

Oct. 27. Letter received and filed. Answer filed.

Oct. 28. Information received that woman has been working in the House of the Holy Comforter with one child, at $6 a month. She kept late hours and was reprimanded. She left, giving no information.

Oct. 31. Letter from Brooklyn Bureau filed.

Nov. 8. Letter to Industrial School, and to woman. Whereabouts of woman unknown. Unstable, needs supervision and discipline. Case closed.

Nov. 10. Case filed.

Nov. 18. Registered letter sent to last address of woman, returned marked not found.

Nov. 27. Visited House of Heavenly Rest—no news. Visited Industrial School—no news. Mother stopped coming to see older child because she became angry at not being allowed to take child out, contrary to rules.

Dec. 4. Various fruitless efforts made to locate her.

Dec. 5. Letter to Central Islip.

Dec. 7. Letter from Infant Asylum filed.

1908

June 6. Woman located through the Industrial School. She took older child home. Earns $10 a week insulating wire for Western Electric Company. Thrown out of employment when company moved to Chicago. Worked in restaurant—$20 a month and two meals a day; church gives $1 worth of groceries weekly. Lives in furnished rooms without proper air or light; manages to pay $1 arrears rent. Children well, but thin, improperly clothed, bold, uncared for.

1908

June 29. Woman calls saying she has lost employment, as help was being cut down. Youngest child seems melancholy and depressed. For 3 years subjected to bad food, and badly-lighted, ill-ventilated living quarters. Visited and asked to move.

June 30. Woman called. Order for $1 given her. Children in Parochial School; to be sent to the country in August; Society of St. Vincent de Paul to help her. Woman calls. Landlord wants back rent. Can find better rooms; given $2 for these rooms.

July 1. Woman calls. Parish will not help her in her new address as she will be out of the district. $7 rent will be paid for her, and furniture will be given her.

July 2. Express company visited. Arrangements made. $5 paid on rent, 25 cents on trunk. Letters to Insane Hospital and to Society St. Vincent de Paul written. Woman calls.

July 3. Groceries, $1.38, sent. Woman calls. Furniture, $8.91, bought for her. Mattress and pillow, $3.10, bought.

July 6. Expressman seen. Woman visited.

July 7. Visited. Articles bought, 95 cents.

July 8. Letter from State Hospital filed. Table bought for $2.25. Visited. Expressman paid $1.50.

July 10. Visited.

July 11. Groceries sent, $1.50. Woman called. Has been laid off.

July 13. Woman calls.

July 15. Visited. Rooms untidy. Friend promises to give her $2 monthly.

July 17. Information received that furniture has been secured for woman.

July 18. Expressman notified to call for furniture. Woman writes that she cannot call at office because face is swollen, and eyes black, due to bite of insect. Visited. She had no money and only a few potatoes; 50 cents given.

July 20. Woman called. Given $1.50.

July 22. Woman called. Half day's work provided.

July 23. Letter written to Amityville.

July 25. Reply received saying woman and two children can be received. Visited. Woman called. Given 50 cents. $13 sent to Amityville for board.

July 27. Accompanied woman and children to station.

July 28. Letter received from Amityville saying they had arrived.

July 29. Expressman paid $2 for his trouble.

July 30. Woman writes grateful letter.

Aug. 1. Bill from Amityville for board $13.90.

Aug. 3. Bill paid.

Aug. 7. Supervisor consulted. August rent to be paid.

Aug. 8. Inquired whether woman could remain longer at Amityville; negative reply received.

Aug. 10. Woman called. Letter written to Manhattan Trade School asking them to receive woman and charge her wages to the Charity Organization Society; $7 rent given her.

1908

Aug. 14. Woman called. Her church visited. Trade School wages paid, $2.10.

Aug. 17. Woman called. Bed spring bought for her, $3.50.

Aug. 19. Woman called; children called; expressman called. Groceries given, $1.72.

Aug. 20. Woman calls. Agent for Society St. Vincent de Paul calls, gives woman $1 for food.

Aug. 21. Letter from Manhattan Trade School.

Aug. 22. Woman calls. Wages paid $3.50.

Aug. 28. Trade School writes. Woman paid $2.80.

Sept. 2. Committee considers case. September rent to be paid.

Sept. 5. Letter received. Woman called. Paid wages $3.50, $7 rent and $2, the monthly gift of a friend.

Sept. 12. Woman called. Paid wages $2.70.

Sept. 19. Woman called. Paid $3.50 wages.

Sept. 26. Woman called. Paid $3.50 wages. Church will give shoes.

Oct. 3. Woman called. Paid $3.50 wages. Asks to have rent paid.

Oct. 5. Letter from friend asking report on the case. Report sent; $2 given woman.

Oct. 6. Committee decided to pay rent.

Oct. 7. Woman called. Is receiving help from church. Has the toothache. Given $7 for rent.

Oct. 8. Visited Trade School. Good report; woman soon to be able to do outside work, needs a machine for home work.

Oct. 9. Superintendent asked to supply machine.

Oct. 10. Letter written to Singer Co. Woman called. Given clothing for herself and children. Paid $2.80 wages.

Oct. 17. Older child called. Society St. Vincent de Paul has provided work for mother. $3.50 wages paid.

Oct. 23. Woman called. Still receiving $1 a week from St. Vincent de Paul. Given clothing. Paid $2.80 wages.

Oct. 31. Woman called. $3.50 wages paid.

Nov. 7. Woman called. Paid $2 pension. Paid $2.80 wages.

Nov. 9. Letter from friend.

Nov. 10. Committee decides to give part of rent.

Nov. 11. Letter to woman filed.

Nov. 12. Older child called. Paid toward rent $3.50.

Nov. 14. Older child called. Paid wages $3.50.

Nov. 21. Older child called. Paid wages $3.50.

Nov. 25. Thanksgiving dinner provided.

Nov. 27. Visited.

Nov. 28. Paid wages $3.50.

Dec. 4. Verbal report to friend.

Dec. 5. Verbal report from friend. Woman called. Younger child ill. Paid pension $2. Paid wages $2.80. Woman calls. Dispensary has treated younger child and she needs milk. Kitchen permit for milk and one dozen eggs, 30 cents given her.

1908

Dec. 7. Visited. Younger child in bed, better. To have adenoids removed.

Dec. 8. Committee decides to give rent.

Dec. 10. Woman advised to take child to N. Y. Hospital for operation. Child admitted. Told that lost time would be made up. Given $3.50 toward rent.

Dec. 11. Letter written to Society asking for bed clothes. Woman calls.

Dec. 12. Woman calls. $3.50 wages.

Dec. 17. Report received that child is in hospital, not yet operated upon.

Dec. 19. Older child called. Paid wages $3.50. Younger child has tonsils removed.

Dec. 23. Given clothing. Christmas dinner.

Dec. 24. Given two coats.

Dec. 26. Older child called. Paid $2.80 wages.

1909

Jan. 2. Paid wages $3.50.

Jan. 7. Bill N. Y. Kitchen, 42 cents. Woman called. Given $3.50 toward rent, $2 pension and wages $3.50.

Jan. 11. Visited.

Jan. 16. Older child called. Paid $3.40 wages.

Jan. 23. Given $3.50 toward rent.

Jan. 30. Paid wages $3.50.

Feb. 6. Given $5.75 toward rent. Given wages $3.10.

Feb. 10. Bill from N. Y. Kitchen for $1.68.

Feb. 15. Paid wages $3.50.

Feb. 16. N. Y. Kitchen bill paid.

Feb. 19. Woman called. Older child sick. Dispensary advises milk and eggs. Eggs, 84 cents, given.

Feb. 20. Kitchen permit given for both children. Paid wages $3.15.

Feb. 24. Older child has adenoids and enlarged tonsils.

Feb. 25. Trade School communicated with.

Feb. 26. Younger child called. Mother sick. Paid $3.50 wages.

Mar. 1. Visited. Woman called.

Mar. 2. Letter to dispensary asking diagnosis.

Mar. 3. Visited. Woman sick in bed with grippe.

Mar. 4. Kitchen bill received for $2.10. Younger child called. Mother better. Given eggs, 60 cents.

Mar. 6. Both children called. Given wages, $3.50, mother would have earned if she had not been sick.

Mar. 8. Older child called. Mother has pleurisy, wants doctor.

Mar. 9. District nurse calls.

Mar. 10. Paid $7 rent. Nurse and doctor visit her. $1.22 paid for nourishment.

Mar. 13. Report sent. Letter from dispensary filed. Two dozen eggs, 60 cents, given. Paid wages $3.50.

Mar. 15. Older child called.

Mar. 17. Telephone message.

1909

Mar. 20. Older child called. Paid wages $3.50. Letter filed.
Mar. 23. Arrangements for woman to go to Spring Valley.
April 3. Milk, $3.36.
April 8. Returns from Spring Valley, better.
April 10. Two dozen eggs, 60 cents.
April 16. Two dozen eggs, 60 cents.
April 17. Older child called. Given $3.50 wages.
April 23. Two dozen eggs, 60 cents.
April 24. Older child called. Given $3.50.
April 30. Woman called. Given $5. Summer work to be found for her in the country.
May 1. Older child given $3.50 wages.
May 8. Bill from N. Y. Kitchen $1.26. Woman called. Paid wages $3.50.
May 13. Summer work found in country with children. Given $12 cash.
May 15. Woman called. $4.50 wages paid.
May 22. Woman called. Paid $2.80 wages. Given clothing, 69 cents.
May 28. Both children called.
May 29. Both children taken to picnic. Given $3.50 wages. Given $3.50 toward rent.
June 2. Woman called. Given laundry permit. Eggs, $3.
June 4. N. Y. Kitchen 84 cents.
June 8. Older child called. Paid wages 70 cents.
June 11. Both children taken on picnic.
June 17. Telephone message. Letter to woman.
June 18. Older child called. Given clothing.
June 19. Visited. Woman called. Letter to ——.
June 22. Letter answered, woman requested to come on certain day to go to work.
June 23. Woman leaves for her work.
June 25. Letter from woman filed.
June 30. Letter to woman filed.
July 1. Eggs, $1.20, paid. Rent, $7, paid.
July 6. Good report received from employer.
July 14. Letter from woman.
July 31. Unable to do the work. To return to the city.
Aug. 2. Woman dissatisfied with accommodations. Children need shoes. Rent, $7, paid.
Aug. 3. Woman to return to city. Gives slack work as reason. Has earned $14.50.
Aug. 12. Visited.
Aug. 13. Woman called.
Aug. 24. Visited.
Aug. 26. Woman called.
Sept. 2. Older child called.
Sept. 4. Older child called.
Sept. 8. Older child called. Mother cannot get steady work, needs help. Committee decides to give $3.

1909

Sept. 9. Woman called. Given laundry permit.

Sept. 11. Woman called. Paid 50 cents in advance for work.

Sept. 13. Younger child called and returned money as there was no work.

Sept. 14. Woman called. Given $3 for rent. Looking for work.

Sept. 22. Visited. Working in candy factory, $3 a week.

Oct. 6. Older child called. Given $2 pension.

Oct. 15. Visited parochial school, children attend very irregularly, should be committed.

Oct. 16. Older child called. Admonished.

Oct. 21. School visited. Attendance better.

Oct. 23. Visited. Rooms untidy.

Nov. 3. Older child called. Given $2 pension. Thanksgiving dinner provided.

Nov. 27. Visited. House untidy. Older child in bed.

Dec. 4. Visited.

Dec. 6. Younger child called. Paid $2 pension.

Dec. 8. Older child called. Mother has sprained ankle.

Dec. 9. Visited. Ankle better. Thinks she will lose job. Was thinking of giving it up herself as it was too hard.

Dec. 11. Letter to dispensary. Reply received. Visited. Groceries sent.

Dec. 13. Visited. Ankle better.

Dec. 17. Visited. Position in candy factory lost. Coal, food, groceries sent.

Dec. 22. Woman called. Letter from friend. Christmas dinner provided.

Dec. 24. Report to friend.

Dec. 28. Visited for work.

Dec. 31. Visited.

1910

Jan. 4. Paid groceries, $3.03. Older child called. Mother has worked several days but has only $1 toward the rent and wants the rest. Committee decided to give it.

Jan. 5. Older child called. Given $5.50 toward the rent. Woman working. Younger child asked to call at dispensary.

Jan. 6. Younger child taken to dispensary, has chorea. Mother displeased because child is taken to wrong dispensary.

Jan. 18. Visited. Woman working. Children at school.

Jan. 24. Visited, 9 A. M. Woman and both children in one bed, all windows closed. Woman has given up work as it did not pay her well enough to continue.

Feb. 3. Visited. Woman doing day's work.

Feb. 4. Older child called. Given $3 toward rent.

Feb. 26. Visited. They have moved, leaving no address.

Feb. 28. Visited parochial school. Children irregular in attendance. Cannot locate family.

Mar. 1. Letter written asking address.

Mar. 18. Effort made to locate. No success.

April 6. Effort made to locate. No success.

1910
April 14. Effort made to locate. No success.
April 26. Case closed.
May 6. Another effort made to locate. No success.
May 13. Older child seen on the street. Furnished an address. Mother is doing odd jobs. Moved because the weather was warm.

Charity Record—Sarah P. (see page 5)

1903 Harry, an idiot son, discharged from Randall's Island.
1906
Jan. . Harry recommitted to Randall's Island.
Feb. 21. Woman's case examined. Commitment of all the children asked.
Feb. 22. Doctor examined mother. Diagnosis—heart disease and tuberculosis.
Feb. 23. Sam, a feeble-minded son, "with fits," sent to —— Orphan Asylum. Leon, a feeble-minded son, referred to Bureau of Dependent Adults.
Feb. 25. Leon sent to Randall's Island. Discharged from Randall's Island as all right.
April 13. Mother at Bedford Sanitarium, tuberculosis.
April 16. Application for commitment of Hannah, a normal girl, dismissed. Sam and Leon both at Randall's Island.
April 19. Letter and visit.
April 23. Mother called for aid.
April 24. Mother called for aid. Case discussed with Mr. Bauer.
April 25. Sam taken home from Randall's Island.
May 2. Letter.
May 9. Visited.
May 15. Woman calls; obstinate, refuses offer of Orphan Asylum to board out Sam and Hannah.
May 21. Letter. Application for commitment of Sam and Hannah.
June 12. Mother sent to Montefiore Home; Hannah sent to Orphan Asylum. They board her out at Clara de Hirsch Home and Sam out in family.
June 29. Mother calls, referred back from Montefiore Home. Received from discharged patients fund $10, and from Charity Society $2.
July 5. Mother calls, asking aid with rent.
July 9. Visited.
July 11. Visited. Two children boarded out; two on Randall's Island.
July 12. Mother examined by doctor. Diagnosis, tuberculosis; referred B. D. A.
July 16. Mother refuses letter to Mr. Meeks.
Aug. 19. Appeal from woman who boards one of the children for help for mother.
Oct. 22. Cash $2.
Oct. 23. Visited. Woman in bed at 8.30 and refuses to see visitor. Aid given $2.

1906

Oct. 25. Woman told that she must make an effort to support herself as —— Charity Society cannot go on taking care of a single individual.

1907

Feb. 9. Mother takes Sam and Hannah home. Her mind seems affected.

Feb. 10. Letter from Mr. Bauer.

Feb. 13. Woman calls for aid. All children except Leon at home. Mother tries to get them committed; Orphan Asylum refuses to accept them again. Sam sent to H. S. G. S. Mother insists on having Leon discharged from Randall's Island.

Feb. 18. Hannah sent to S. P. C. C.; Leon to Bellevue.

Feb. 20. Mother insists on having Hannah, who is in the Clara de Hirsch Home. Letter to Mr. Bauer relative to Hannah.

Mar. 14. Claims Harry has tuberculosis.

Mar. 19. Mother has called several times. She refuses to use card given her for medical examination for herself and the boy whom she claims to be tubercular.

Mar. 18. Aid given.

Mar. 20. Leon again committed to Randall's Island. Harry in Brooklyn with aunt; Hannah sleeping in bed with mother who has tuberculosis. Whole family in one room; danger of infection.

Mar. 21. Woman calls at office. Letter given for medical examination for herself and Harry. Arrangements made to move family to two rooms. $5.

Mar. 25. Woman examined; no evidence of tuberculosis. Harry has tuberculosis. Rent for new rooms, $12, and $3 a week for living expenses offered woman. Refuses to take it, demands $5 a week. Hannah and Sam call in the afternoon; given shoes and supplies and $5 extra for furniture. Visitor telephones that woman paid deposit on $15 rooms and that she is dissatisfied with $10 for furniture; $12 is final for rent.

Mar. 26. Woman forbidden to come to office unless she obeys.

Mar. 27. Letter from woman requesting increase in allowance in living expenses.

Mar. 28. Calls with entire family. Hannah very rude and impertinent. Woman refuses offer of $2, demands $5. Given $5. Demands furniture.

April 1. Woman calls; says she has rented an apartment for $15. Granted $13 a month for rent, $3 for living expenses and $15 for furniture.

April 4. Receives weekly allowance $3.

April 8. Woman calls at office. Receives rent and supplies, $28.

April 9. A remittance of $5 given by a friend for woman.

April 11. Woman calls. Given weekly allowance and supplies, $3.

April 18. Woman calls. Given bed clothing, quilts, shoes and milk for two weeks, $3.

1907

April 25. Woman calls. Given weekly allowance, $3.

April 26. Woman calls. Although refused admission to —— she pushes her way in. Complains that she is not receiving proper attention. Wants more help. Wants Harry admitted to Montefiore Home thinking he has tuberculosis. Hannah in school, does housework at home. Sam at home again. Leon should be transferred to Rome, but she refuses to allow him to go. $3 a week is continued. Order for clothing, bedding, shoes for herself and girl, jumpers for herself and boy given. Milk and $3 given.

May 2. Given order for two weeks' milk. Given $3.

May 9. Has applied at Montefiore Home for son. Demands to be reimbursed for carfares. Given $3.

May 4. Calls for rent. Check sent for $13.

May 10. Order sent for shoes for Harry.

May 14. Full supplies given.

May 15. Rent, weekly allowance, shoes, $17.50.

May 23. Given $4.50.

May 30. Demand for money to buy shoes for girl refused; given weekly allowance, $3.

June 5. Weekly allowance paid, $3.

June 6. Various letters. Mr. Bauer writes for Harry to be readmitted to Montefiore Home.

June 11. Paid $3.

June 14. Rent paid, $13.

June 15. Paid $3.

June 18. Paid $3.

June 20. Hannah to be sent to country by Board of Education. $3.

June 27. Paid $3.

July 3. Advised to make Hannah go to work, but she refuses as Hannah has been in school and needs rest. Living expenses to be reduced to $2.

July 4. Paid $6.

July 16. Woman calls several times a week; very troublesome. Telephoned Montefiore Home; Harry has bronchitis. Four children at home. Woman refuses to have Hannah work as the United Hebrew Charities should support her. To receive $3 weekly, as usual. Rent and $1 given at once. $13.

July 18. Woman calls. Demands living expenses. She is given $2 as she already has received $1. She refuses to take it.

July 25. Woman placed on the recurrent list for $3 to be given bi-monthly. Paid $5.

July 22. Woman calls daily at main office, demanding $3 and refusing to accept $2 unless carfare amounting to $1.20, spent in calling at the main office, be returned. $2 sent her brought back by her boy.

1907

Aug. 16. Placed on recurrent list. Check for rent sent, $13.

Aug. 22. Check for $5 sent; woman returns it.

Sept. 3. Woman calls and demands shoes for boy and $6 which she says United Hebrew Charities owes her.

Sept. 13. Woman writes for rent.

Sept. 19. Rent paid, $13.

During succeeding intervals woman is paid $13 monthly for rent, and $6 bi-monthly for living expenses. She complains after a time that she has lost a week by that arrangement.

1908

Mar. 2. Woman given $3 extra for week she lost.

Mar. 20. Case re-investigated. Woman very excited; has complained that $12 monthly is not enough for living expenses. Threatens to appeal to District Attorney Jerome who, she claims, will see that she receives increase. At suggestion that Hannah be sent to work, she becomes violent; says she is weak and dependent upon Hannah. Seems of unsound mind.

Aug. 31. Rent and $3 weekly recommended for continuation.

Dec. 2. Letter from Jerome requesting information about the family.

Dec. 4. Letter written to Jerome.

Dec. 8. Letter received from Jerome.

1909

Feb. 25. Pension recommended to be continued, as woman refuses to take Hannah out of school.

Mar. 31. Woman refuses information to special visitor on the plea that United Hebrew Charities is bothering her too much. Recently $6 check held pending investigation.

April 23. Letter from woman complaining that she has not received living expenses.

April 25. Visited; not at home.

April 27. Check for rent and the withheld living expenses sent, $19. Ordered to continue until July when Hannah must go to work. Visitor offers her living expenses—she refuses to receive it. Woman visited several times before, doors locked. Woman asked to come to office, does not come. Complains that she is starving and begging from neighbors. Refuses provisions given her at Christmas and refuses to take $3 unless entire month's rent and allowance are given. Hannah refuses to go to work. Expects to graduate in June and then study stenography and typewriting.

April 30. $3 offered; refused because dated 30th. Wanted check dated 29th. Refused cash.

May 3. Clothes and shoes for Sam given. $3 to be sent weekly.

May 4. Check sent, $3.

May 12. Check, $3.

May 18. Check, $13.

May 26. Check, $3.

1909

June 3. House agent says woman refuses to pay rent. Case reported. Check sent, $3.

June 8. Check held for visitor's report. Check sent, $3.

June 17. Visited to find why rent was not paid. Woman said she had not received it so could not pay. Had received it herself at office. Told that she could not have expenses after July 1. Replied that I might "mind my own business as she could look out for herself." Hannah was impertinent. $5.

June 23. Visited to deliver check for $3. Woman refused to receive it.

June 24. Check for $13 given. Woman refused to receive it. In future check to be sent to landlord.

June 30. Check, $3.

For twenty weeks check sent regularly. To be discontinued after January 1st, as Hannah must work.

Dec. 11. Woman complains to Department of Charities that she has not had expenses for two weeks.

Dec. 22. Department of Charities writes that woman has come again and again asking aid and trying to get children committed.

1910

Jan. 10. Family visited.

Feb. 18. Woman and Sam arraigned before Justice Wyatt. Boy ordered to Randall's Island; mother to Bellevue. Hannah sent to Clara de Hirsch Home. Given letter to United Hebrew Charities.

Feb. 28. Woman asks assistance from the Free Synagogue Society.

Mar. 2. Report that woman was kept at Bellevue only one day and discharged to brother.

Mar. 16. Visited. Woman somewhat humble. Hannah arrogant. Will not leave High School (Bronx) unless course in stenography is paid for. Leon at Gerry Society. Discharged from Randall's Island as cured. Will go to mother.

www.ingramcontent.com/pod-product-compliance
Lightning Source LLC
LaVergne TN
LVHW021424110826
845150LV00007B/2067

9781425508227